WRITE SOURCE

SkillsBook

EDITING AND PROOFREADING PRACTICE

. . . a resource of student activities
to accompany *Write Source*

WRITE SOURCE®

GREAT SOURCE EDUCATION GROUP
a Houghton Mifflin Company
Wilmington, Massachusetts

A Few Words About the *Write Source SkillsBook*

Before you begin . . .

The *SkillsBook* provides you with opportunities to practice editing and proofreading skills presented in the *Write Source* text. It contains guidelines, examples, and models to help you complete your work in the *SkillsBook*.

Each *SkillsBook* activity includes a brief introduction to the topic and examples showing how to complete that activity. You will be directed to the page numbers in the handbook for additional information and examples. The "Proofreading Activities" focus on punctuation, the mechanics of writing, usage, and spelling. The "Sentence Activities" provide practice in sentence combining and in correcting common sentence problems. The "Language Activities" highlight each of the eight parts of speech.

The Next Step Most activities include a next step at the end of the exercise. The purpose of The Next Step is to provide ideas for follow-up work that will help you apply what you have learned in your own writing.

Authors: Pat Sebranek and Dave Kemper

Printed in the United States of America

International Standard Book Number: 978-0-669-51819-1 (student edition)

9 10 11 12 13 -1689- 14 13 12 11 10

4500234275

International Standard Book Number: 978-0-669-51824-5 (teacher's edition)

6 7 8 9 10 -POO- 10 09 08

Table of Contents
Proofreading Activities

Marking Punctuation

Editing for Mechanics

Sentence Activities

Sentence Variety

Language Activities

Nouns

Pronouns

Verbs

Proofreading Activities

Every activity in this section includes sentences that need to be checked for punctuation, mechanics, or usage. Most of the activities also include helpful *Write Source* references. In addition, The Next Step, which is at the end of most activities, encourages follow-up practice of certain skills.

End Punctuation 1

There are three ways to end a sentence. You may use a **period**, a **question mark**, or an **exclamation point**. (See *Write Source* pages 479 and 480.)

Examples

Animals *talk* in many ways.

Do you understand your dog's barking?

It's raining cats and dogs!

Directions Put the correct end punctuation in the sentences below. You will also need to add a capital letter at the beginning of each sentence. The first sentence has been done for you.

1   did you know that many animals have their own language

2   dolphins "talk" by making clicking sounds a dolphin can make as

3   many as 700 clicks in one second bees "talk" by flying in patterns

4   like dancing they tell other bees where to find flowers.

5   some animals even "speak" in ways that humans might

6   understand have you ever noticed that dogs have different barks a

7   dog barks one way when someone is at the door and another way

8   when it is hurt

9   a gorilla named Koko has gone one step further she actually

10   talks to humans she has learned a sign language when a kitten

11   bit Koko, she made signs to say, "Teeth visit gorilla." it is not the

12   way you would say it, but you know what she meant "Ouch"

End Punctuation 2

This activity gives you practice using end punctuation. (See *Write Source* pages 479 and 480.)

Examples

Years ago, a cat named Napoleon became famous.

Do you know why?

He could predict the weather!

Directions ▶ Put the correct end punctuation in the sentences below. You'll also need to add a capital letter at the beginning of each sentence. The first sentence has been done for you.

1 Napoleon lived in Baltimore with his owner. in the summer

2 of 1930, it didn't rain for a long time one day, Napoleon's owner

3 called the newspapers and said that rain was on the way they

4 didn't believe him, but Napoleon's owner knew better Napoleon

5 was napping with one front paw stretched out and his head on

6 the floor whenever Napoleon did that, it soon began to rain

7 what do you think happened yes it poured and poured from

8 then on, the newspapers printed Napoleon's weather forecasts he

9 was right as often as the human weather forecaster don't you

10 wish you had a cat like Napoleon at your house

The Next Step People commonly ask questions and make comments about the weather. Write at least five sentences related to the weather. Be sure to use the correct end punctuation!

Commas Between Items in a Series 1

Commas are used between words or phrases in a series. (See *Write Source* page 482.)

Example

I have pen pals in *Australia*, *Greece*, and *Ireland*.

 **Directions**   In the paragraph below, add commas between items in a series. The first sentence has been done for you.

1   Antarctica, Europe, and Australia are continents. Australia

2   is the only country that takes up a whole continent. Australia

3   has many large deserts, some coastal rain forests, and the world's

4   largest coral reef. The reef is called the Great Barrier Reef is

5   1,200 miles long and is on the northeast coast. Australia is

6   surrounded by the Indian Ocean, Coral Sea and Tasman Sea.

7   Kangaroos, kookaburras, and dingoes are just a few of the unusual

8   animals that live in Australia. Queensland, Victoria, and New

9   South Wales are three of Australia's states. Queensland is the size

10   of California, Arizona, New Mexico, and Texas combined. Australia

11   has diamonds, gold, copper, and other gems and minerals.

The Next Step Write four sentences of your own about Australia or about another country. Use commas in a series in at least two of your sentences.

Commas Between Items in a Series 2

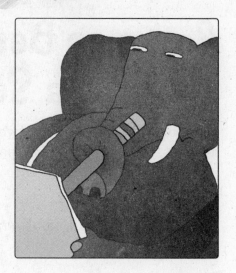

Commas are used between words or phrases in a series. (See *Write Source* page 482.)

Example

I have seen elephants *at zoos*, *at circuses*, and *at safari parks*.

 **Directions** In the sentences below, add commas between items in a series. The first sentence has been done for you.

1 Elephants are not just huge, heavy, and clumsy. They can do

2 amazing things. Everyone knows that elephants use their trunks

3 to hold things, take up water, and throw dust. Siri, a zoo elephant,

4 held a rock in her trunk, scratched it on the floor, and drew designs.

5 The zookeeper gave Siri a pencil and paper, and she kept drawing.

6   Elephants eat grass, shrubs, branches, leaves, bark, roots, and

7 fruit. Sometimes they knock down trees, rip off their bark, and dig

8 up their roots. Wild elephants eat 600-800 pounds of food a day.

9   Elephants' sharp tusks, long trunks, and crushing feet can be

10 dangerous. Elephants also can be intelligent, protective, and gentle.

11 Once a baby elephant got hurt. The herd followed the leader, found

12 a park ranger, and led the ranger back to the baby elephant.

Commas in Compound Sentences

Commas are used between independent clauses that are joined by words such as *and, but, or, nor, for, so,* and *yet.* (See *Write Source* page 482.)

Example

Bats sleep all day, *but* they eat mosquitoes and other insects all night.

 **Directions** ▶ **In the sentences below, add commas between independent clauses. The first sentence has been done for you.**

1   Hundreds of years ago, the whole United States was

2   covered with forests, grassy fields, and deserts, so animals lived

3   everywhere! But there are more people today, and they have

4   built homes, malls, and parking lots where animals used to live.

5   Because of these changes, many animals left urbanized areas, but

6   some have been able to adapt to cities and have stayed.

7   If you have a cat, put a bell on its collar, or it may sneak

8   up on wild animals. Put water in a birdbath, or other shallow

9   container for birds. Plant a berry bush, and it will provide food

10   for wild animals. Buy a bat house at the hardware store

11   , and encourage this helpful insect eater to keep your yard

12   mosquito-free.

Commas to Set Off Introductory Phrases and Clauses

Commas can be used to set off long phrases and clauses that come before the main part of the sentence. (See *Write Source* page 484.)

Example

In the last few years, most cities have developed recycling programs.

Directions Each sentence below starts with a long phrase or clause that modifies the rest of the sentence. Add a comma after each phrase or clause. The first sentence has been done for you.

1. If you want to help the environment, you can recycle many things.

2. Because glass never wears out it can be recycled forever.

3. Though it's hard to believe people have been recycling glass for more than 3,000 years!

4. At most recycling stations you'll find a bin for aluminum cans.

5. Even with all the different kinds some plastic can be recycled, too.

6. Before you recycle plastic you must separate the different kinds.

7. To avoid polluting the environment car oil is recycled.

8. Because there are many uses for tires people recycle them, also.

The Next Step Write a letter to your school principal (or your city council) about recycling. Begin several sentences with long introductory phrases or clauses. Be sure to use commas correctly. (See the sample business letter on *Write Source* page 244.)

Commas in Dates and Addresses

Commas are used to set off the different parts in addresses and dates. (See *Write Source* page 484.)

Example

My best friend's address is 800 West Street, Bonne Terre, Missouri 63982. He moved here from Boston, Massachusetts, on August 4, 2004.

 **Directions** ▶ **Add commas where they are needed in the addresses and dates below.**

1   My sister and I wanted to go to a Disney theme park for

2   our vacation—maybe in Orlando Florida or Anaheim California.

3   Instead we will go camping in one of our state parks. To start

4   planning, we sent for information from the Ste. Genevieve

5   Convention and Visitors Bureau 66 South Main Street Ste.

6   Genevieve Missouri 63670 on January 31 2006. Our mailman

7   delivered a large packet of brochures on February 8 2006.

8   After looking them over, Mom decided we should camp in Lake

9   Wappapello State Park near Williamsville Missouri. She says we'll

10   camp for a whole week starting on June 4 2006. That means

11   we won't have to break camp until June 11 2006. We'll swim

12   and fish and tell ghost stories around the campfire. Some of the

13   towns we'll drive through on our vacation are Flat River Missouri;

14   Farmington Missouri; and Greenville Missouri. We can't wait to go!

Commas to Keep Numbers Clear

Commas are placed between hundreds, thousands, millions, and so on. (See *Write Source* page 484.)

Example

The planet Mercury is 36,000,000 miles from the sun.
(You may also write the number this way: 36 million.)

 **Add commas to numbers where they are needed in the sentences below.**

1. The surface of the sun is a sizzling 11000 degrees Fahrenheit.

2. The center of the sun burns even hotter at 27000000 degrees!

3. Even though it is 93000000 miles away from Earth, the sun can heat some places on our planet to around 136 degrees Fahrenheit.

4. Pluto takes 90520 days to revolve around the sun once. With a "year" that long, summer vacation would last 22630 days!

5. Because gravity is weak on Mars, a 2000-pound elephant would weigh only 760 pounds.

6. On Jupiter, because of strong gravity, the same elephant would weigh 5060 pounds.

7. Venus and Earth are about the same size. Earth's diameter is 7926 miles, and Venus's is 7519 miles.

8. Jupiter is the largest planet in our solar system with a humongous diameter of 88736 miles.

Commas to Set Off Interruptions

Commas are used to set off a word or a phrase that interrupts the main thought of a sentence. (See *Write Source* page 486.)

Example

Eurasian reindeer are small. The male, in fact, is only four feet high at the shoulder.

Directions ▶ **Insert commas as needed in the sentences below.**

1. Reindeer are indeed strong animals.

2. A reindeer can pull twice its own weight actually on a sled.

3. Moreover reindeer can carry heavy burdens and riders.

4. These deer have been very important to northern people. Until recently, Laplanders as a matter of fact depended completely on the reindeer for their livelihood.

5. Reindeer after all can provide meat, milk, clothing, and transportation.

6. Reindeer feed on various plants. For example they eat grasses in the summer and lichens in the winter.

7. North America has its own version of the reindeer, called caribou. Caribou however are larger than their Eurasian cousins.

Commas in Direct Address

Commas are used to separate the person being spoken to from the rest of the sentence. (See *Write Source* page 486.)

Example

"Alicia, if you could travel anywhere in the world, where would you go?"

 **Insert commas where needed in the following sentences.**

1. "I want to go to Mongolia Ms. Baines."

2. "No way Alicia," said Maxie.

3. "Yeah, Alicia come on. Where do you really want to go?" asked Larry.

4. "Class let Alicia tell us about her dream," said Ms. Baines.

5. "I read about an 18-day trip to Mongolia Ms. Baines."

6. "Larry you get to ride horses for nine of those days!"

7. "You camp along the way Maxie and you learn how people lived way

   back in the days of Genghis Khan."

8. "What else do you get to do Alicia?" asked Ms. Baines.

9. "You eventually meet the Reindeer People in a remote mountain valley

   Ms. Baines. They're a nomad group who herd reindeer."

10. "You sit around campfires Maxie and listen to stories and eat 'horhog,'

    whatever that is."

11. "Gosh, Alicia it was sounding good until that part," piped up Larry.

Commas to Set Off Appositives

Commas are also used to set off appositives. (See *Write Source* page 488.)

Example

Bamboo, *a tall grass,* is used to build houses.
(The appositive *a tall grass* renames *bamboo*.)

 **Directions** Add a comma before and after (if needed) each appositive in the sentences below. The first sentence has been done for you.

1. Hogans, houses made of logs and mud, are built by the Navajo.

2. Igloos shelters made of packed snow are used by the Inuit.

3. Tepees cone-shaped tents are made from buffalo skins.

4. A tepee can easily be moved on a travois a sledlike carrier.

5. Yurts large domed tents made of skins or felt are shaped like igloos.

6. Yurts are built by people in Mongolia an area in Asia.

7. A laavu a tent much like a tepee is a shelter used in Lapland.

8. Lapland an area in northern Europe is cold and snowy.

9. In Hong Kong, some people live on sampans small houseboats.

10. The bones of mammoths mammals that are now extinct were used to build houses in the Stone Age.

14

 **Directions** ▶ Add an appositive to each of the following sentences. Begin your appositive where you see the caret (∧). You may add any word or phrase you like, as long as it renames the noun that comes before it. Use commas correctly. The first one has been done for you.

1. Our teacher ∧ read a story aloud.

Our teacher, Ms. Garrett, read a story aloud.

2. My favorite book ∧ was checked out of the library.

_____

_____

3. Our principal ∧ came to our class.

_____

_____

The Next Step Now complete the sentences started below by adding an appositive and other words. The first one has been done for you.

1. My favorite place *, Florida, is where my grandparents live.*

2. Our school _____

_____

3. Our science book _____

_____

4. My hometown _____

_____

Commas in Letter Writing

Commas are placed after the greeting in a friendly letter and after the closing in all letters. (See *Write Source* page 488.)

Example

Dear Sarah**,**

    I can't wait till your visit, can you? When does your train . . .

Your best friend**,**
Maria

 **Make the necessary corrections in the following exercises. If commas are already used correctly, write "C" on the blank.**

1. ____ Dear President Bush:

    It has come to my . . .

Sincerely;

Martin Baines

2. ____ Dear Grandma,

    Thanks for the . . .

Love

Susie

3. ____ Dear Mrs. Settler,

    I hope you . . .

Sincerely,

Susie

4. ____ Dear Marty!

    How are you? I . . .

Friends,

Buzzy

5. ____ Dear Director:

    I am a student . . .

Yours truly,

Sally Farthing

6. ____ Dear Pedro

    For the next . . .

Your friend

Paco

Commas Practice

Directions ▶ Add commas correctly in the sentences below.

1   "Yuri what did you decide to write about?"

2   "I didn't decide yet Darius. How about you?"

3   "I picked a subject yesterday as a matter of fact. After I read

4   some magazines I decided to write about climbing Mount Everest."

5   Mount Everest the tallest mountain in the world is 29035

6   feet high. This majestic mountain is near Kathmandu Nepal on

7   the Tibetan border. On May 29 1953 Edmund Hillary and Tenzing

8   Norgay became the first climbers to reach the summit of Mount

9   Everest. Norgay was a Sherpa a member of a Tibetan group who

10   live in the high altitudes. They are expert mountain-climbing

11   guides. Sherpas in fact helped the National Geographic 50th

12   Anniversary Everest Expedition to the summit on May 25 2002.

13   Although climbing the mountain was hard enough the group also

14   made a documentary film along the way. You can write to the

15   National Geographic Society 1145 17th Street N.W., Washington

16   D.C. 20036, for more information about the expedition.

End Punctuation and
Comma Review

 **Directions** ► Put commas and the correct end punctuation in the sentences below. Also capitalize the first letter of each sentence.

1   have you ever seen turtles the only reptiles with a shell in

2   pet shops in the streets or on logs and rocks at the edge of a

3   river or pond they were probably painted turtles or box turtles

4   some cities and towns have crossing signs that warn drivers not

5   to run over ducks geese or slow-moving turtles

6   there are many different kinds of turtles there are sea

7   turtles desert turtles snapping turtles and others sea turtles are

8   huge and they can live for 100 years in the United States desert

9   tortoises live in the deserts of the Southwest these turtles could

10   become extinct soon because cows are eating their homes they live

11   under shrubs that cows like to eat can you guess how snapping

12   turtles got their name when bothered they will try to bite

13   anything that moves so watch out snapping turtles can weigh as

14   much as 200 pounds some people like to make turtle soup using

15   these fierce-looking turtles

The Next Step Turtles often fall over on their backs when they try to climb up on something sometimes. They can't get right side up again unless someone helps them. Pretend that you're a turtle, and you're stuck on your back. Write a paragraph about how you feel before and after a human comes along and helps you back onto your feet. Be sure to use each of the three types of end punctuation at least once, and use commas where they are needed.

_____

_____

_____

_____

_____

_____

_____

_____

_____

_____

_____

_____

Apostrophes 1

Apostrophes are used in many different ways. One of the most common uses is making contractions. (See *Write Source* page 490.)

Example

You'd see penguins in Antarctica.
(You + would = You'd)

 **Directions**   In the following sentences, make as many contractions as you can. The first contraction has been done for you. (The number of contractions you can make is indicated in parentheses.)

1. Antarctica is so frozen that people only visit; they ~~do not~~ *don't* live there. *(1)*

2. It is easy to get the Arctic and Antarctica mixed up. *(1)*

3. Here is a way to remember which is which. *(1)*

4. At the North Pole, the Arctic is an ocean that is surrounded by land. *(1)*

5. Antarctica is land that is surrounded by water, and it is at the South Pole. *(2)*

6. Polar bears and seals live on islands of ice in the Arctic, and they are at home there even though it is cold. *(2)*

7. Antarctica is even colder than the Arctic, but the penguins that live there do not seem to mind. *(1)*

The Next Step   Write a message to a friend telling her or him about your trip to Antarctica. Use as many contractions as you can.

Apostrophes 2

Use an apostrophe and *s* to form the possessive of most singular nouns. (See *Write Source* page 490.)

Examples   the dog's food   an owner's manual   the bee's buzzing

The possessive of a singular noun ending in an *s* or a *z* sound may be formed by adding just an apostrophe, unless it is a one-syllable word.

Examples   Dickens' books (or) Dickens's books

Carlos' folder (or) Carlos's folder

James's hobby   Mr. Jones's driveway

 **Write the correct possessive form above each underlined word in the sentences below.**

1. The <u>Arctic</u> cold weather doesn't seem to bother the Inuit people.

2. <u>Canada</u> newest territory, Nunavut, is populated by the Inuit people.

3. The <u>ancestors</u> way of life was based on fishing and hunting.

4. Inuit sled dogs played an important role in this <u>people</u> day-to-day life.

5. A sled <u>dog</u> strength is amazing, as he can pull one and a half times his own weight.

6. The dogs can sniff out a <u>seal</u> breathing hole for the hunters.

7. A sled <u>dog</u> bark is more like a <u>wolf</u> long, sad howl.

8. My dog, Sass, is much quieter than that, but <u>Sass</u> barking does upset my <u>neighbor</u> cat.

Apostrophes 3

Apostrophes may be used to make possessives—
to show ownership. (See *Write Source* pages 490
and 492.)

Example

I think *Mia's* pet is the most unusual one.
(The pet belongs to Mia.)

The *pets'* cages are colorful.
(The cages belong to the pets)

**Each sentence below contains one or two possessive nouns that need an
apostrophe (or an apostrophe *and* an "s"). Add what's needed to make the
possessive form correct. The first sentence has been done for you.**

1. Our teachers husband is an airline pilot.

2. My oldest sisters puppy and my youngest brothers cat tease each other.

3. My fathers boss is from Singapore.

4. Aunt Doris hat flew out the window, and Moms scarf followed it.

5. Uncle Ross laughter could be heard around the block.

6. The bus tires ran over the hat and squashed it.

7. The boys soccer team played the girls soccer team.

8. At the zoo, the elephants cages are huge.

9. The snakes cages are made of glass.

10. All of my classmates art projects are on display.

Directions Under "Singular Possessives," write down the names of four people you know. Imagine that each person has caught a fish Using apostrophes correctly, show that each person owns a fish. Next, think of four pairs of people, and write them under "Plural Possessives." Use apostrophes correctly to show that each pair owns a fish. The first one in each category has been done for you.

Singular Possessives

1. *Joe's fish*

2. _____

3. _____

4. _____

5. _____

Plural Possessives

1. *Joe and Rosa's fish*

2. _____

3. _____

4. _____

5. _____

The Next Step Write a short paragraph in which you use one of your singular possessives and one of your plural possessives from above.

_____

_____

_____

Quotation Marks 1

Use **quotation marks** before and after spoken words. Also use them with words taken directly from a piece of writing. (See *Write Source* page 494.)

Examples

"Rise and shine!" called Mom. The brochure told us that Wyoming has "fishing galore, gorgeous autumn color in the mountains, and breathtaking hiking trails."

Directions ▶ Place quotation marks correctly in the following sentences.

1. I'm very sure that the sun isn't up yet, yawned Bobbie.

2. But we are, said Grandpa. Come on! The fish are waiting.

3. The park newspaper has lots of advice. One paragraph starts out,

   Never leave food open in the campsite overnight.

4. Raccoons and bears can open coolers. Did you know that? asked Midge.

5. I don't want to see that happen! piped up Bobbie.

6. I think raccoons are cute, said Minnie.

7. Not when they're stealing your food, they're not, said Todd.

8. Well, I'm kind of tired of hot dogs anyway, barked Grandpa. Let's catch

   some fish!

9. If the campers catch no fish, the park newspaper has another tip: Visit

   our dining lodge for good home cooking.

"Oh, Oh!" exclaimed Dad.

Quotation Marks 2

Place **quotation marks** around titles of songs, poems, short stories, book chapters, and articles. (See *Write Source* 494.)

Examples

"My Old Kentucky Home" *(song)*   "That New Kid" *(short story)*
"Girl Finds Lost Treasure" *(article)*   "Teeny Tiny Mice" *(poem)*
"The Last Chance" *(book chapter)*

 **Directions**   Insert quotation marks correctly in the following sentences. (Commas and periods go inside quotation marks.)

1. Sarah got scared reading the short story Ghosts in the Doghouse.

2. That magazine article about riding horses, Saddle Up for Adventure, sounds interesting to me.

3. Marcia loves horses, and she wrote two poems about them today:

   My Own Horse and Appaloosa Wind.

4. Reggie asked Mom to read two chapters of the book to him: Old

   Friends and Lifesavers.

5. The headline story in the school newspaper was No New Playground.

6. Casey taught us two songs: On Top of Old Smokey and The Honey Bee.

7. This morning's paper has an article about stray pets: Humane Society

   Shelter Overcrowded.

8. We are assigned to read the next chapter, Uncle Willie, for tomorrow,

   and the one after that, Umbrellas, for Friday.

Hyphens 1

Certain compound words are *always* hyphenated (*off-season* and *off-limits*). Other compound words are written as one word (*offspring* and *offbeat*). In other cases, **hyphens** are used to create single-thought adjectives (*off-and-on* friendship and *off-and-running* start). Hyphens sometimes join a letter to a word.

Example

Randi got a *red-and-white* striped scarf.

He made a *U-turn* with his snowmobile.

 **Directions**   Replace the underlined adjectives with single-thought adjectives from the list to complete the following story. The first one has been done for you.

below-zero	face-to-the-wind	H-shaped	sound-swallowing
bone-chilling	A-frame	never-ending	steam-engine
cattle-herding	heat-trapping	rodeo-like	storm-weary

bone-chilling

1. Despite the <u>cold</u> blizzard, today we're moving the cattle up north.

2. We all wore <u>thermal</u> clothes under our sweaters and jackets.

3. Now, instead of a <u>fun</u> ride, this would be <u>windy, cold</u> work.

4. The barks of the <u>working</u> dogs were lost in the <u>roaring</u> wind.

5. Later, the dogs would return to snug <u>tentlike</u> doghouses.

6. The <u>very cold</u> windchill left riders with fingers growing numb.

7. <u>Steamy</u> snorts rose above the heads of the cattle.

8. The rolling North Dakota prairie disappeared into <u>endless</u> white.

9. Finally, the outlines of the <u>familiar</u> barns appeared in the distance.

10. <u>Tired</u> riders could now turn their backs to the wind and head for home.

Hyphens 2

Hyphens are used to divide words at the end of a line and to form new words beginning with the prefixes *all-*, *ex-*, *great-*, and *self-*. (See *Write Source* page 496.)

Example

Mom baked some hot, buttery **home-made** biscuits with **all-purpose** flour.

Directions Review the rules in *Write Source* about dividing words. Then read the sentences below. If the word at the end of the line is divided correctly, write "C" on the short line. Otherwise, show the correct way to divide or write the word.

____ Emma and I always wash the supper dishes by hand. The autom-

____ atic dishwasher has a broken switch. That seems old-

____ fashioned, but the dishes get clean, and Dad noticed that we do-

____ n' use as much electricity that way. Mom, too, is happy about be-

____ ing earth-friendly. She says the environment needs a few good fri-

____ ends. And do you think we would ever use a garbage dis-

____ posal? No way. Food garbage goes in the compost heap in the ba-

____ ckyard. It makes good fertilizer. All the rabbits in the neighborhood a-

____ gree that we have very tasty homegrown vegetables!

The Next Step Combine the following prefixes and words, using hyphens correctly. Finally, choose two of the words to include in a sentence on your own paper.

ex (plus)	self (plus)	all (plus)
classmate _____	winding _____	star _____
president _____	cleaning _____	around _____

Colons 1

A **colon** is used to introduce a list in a sentence. (See *Write Source* page 498.)

Example

Each student could choose to make a model of one of the following: an adobe house, a tepee, a log cabin, or an igloo.

 **Directions** ▶ Add a colon where one is needed in each sentence below. The first sentence has been done for you.

1. Each model must have these parts: a door or an entrance, one opening to let light in, and one opening to let smoke out.

2. For my igloo, I need these materials a cookie sheet, sugar cubes, and frosting.

3. These three students are making adobe houses Marcia, Jamila, and Josh.

4. Real adobe is made from two ingredients mud and straw.

5. To make a model tepee, you could use the following leather, waxed paper, or felt.

6. A log cabin could be made from these materials rolled-up construction-paper logs, bread-dough logs, or real sticks.

The Next Step Write two questions that call for lists. Then write your own sentence to answer each question. Be sure to use a colon in each answer.

Colons 2

Colons are used after the greeting in a business letter. (See *Write Source* page 498.)

Example

Dear Mr. and Mrs. Zinnen:

Our school has chosen you as honorary . . .

Sincerely,
Martha Ludding

Directions ▶ Write the correct greeting for a business letter to each of the people listed below.

Museum Director   Mr. Garganzola   Ms. Templeton
Dr. O'Leary   Professor Mann   Mrs. Rumsfeld

1. _____   4. _____

2. _____   5. _____

3. _____   6. _____

 **Directions** ▶ Correct the punctuation in the following exercises. Write "C" on the line if everything is correct.

1. ____ Dear Professor Mann;

   I am studying moths in our . . .

   Sincerely,

   Rob Starling

2. ____ Dear Park Ranger,

   Last year my family . . .

   Yours truly,

   Sarah Fast

3. ____ Dear Ms. Cannon:

   I want to do a report on . . .

   Sincerely,

   Bob Lane

4. ____ Dear Sergeant Keats!

   My brother is in your . . .

   Sincerely,

   Maria Reyez

Semicolons

A **semicolon** can be used instead of a comma and a coordinating conjunction to connect two independent clauses. (See *Write Source* page 500.)

Example

It was supposed to snow today, *but* it didn't.

It was supposed to snow today; it didn't.

 **Directions**   In each sentence below, replace the comma and coordinating conjunction with a semicolon. The first sentence has been done for you.

1. A few minutes ago, the sun was shining; yet now it's raining!

2. Todd is all wet, and Terry is, too.

3. They got caught in the rain, but I didn't.

4. They were walking home from school, and the rain started.

5. They were near my house, so they ran for our door.

6. I got home early, so I escaped the rain.

7. They're staying here, and we're doing our homework together.

8. They needed to dry off first, though, for they were getting cold.

9. I gave Todd and Terry some dry clothes, but they didn't fit.

10. They called their mom, and she brought them some clothes.

The Next Step   Write three sentences that use a comma and a coordinating conjunction to connect two independent clauses. (See *Write Source* page 600 for a list of coordinating conjunctions.) Trade papers with a partner. Rewrite each other's sentences, using a semicolon instead of the comma and conjunction.

Italics and Underlining

Italics, *a slanted type,* is used for certain titles and special words. You may also **underline** instead of using italic type. (See *Write Source* page 502.)

Examples

Oliver Twist *(book)*   Air Force One *(presidential plane)*

Celtic Highlands *(CD)*   Big Fish *(DVD)*

Edmund Fitzgerald *(ship)*   Tyrannosaurus rex *(scientific name)*

New York Times *(newspaper)*   This Old House *(TV program)*

Ice Age *(movie)*   bonjour *(non-English word)*

Romeo and Juliet *(play)*   Zoobooks *(magazine)*

 **Directions**   **Correctly underline titles and special words in the sentences below. Remember, not all titles should be underlined.**

1. My dog-loving brother read the book Shiloh by Phyllis Reynolds Naylor.

2. I read One-Eyed Cat by Paula Fox for my book review assignment.

3. "Pirates at Their Own Funeral" is the name of a chapter in Mark

   Twain's The Adventures of Tom Sawyer.

4. Jake asked for the DVD Spiderman for his birthday.

5. The spaceship Apollo 13 was launched on April 11, 1970.

6. Grandma says she read about it in the Indianapolis Star newspaper.

7. The movie Apollo 13 with Tom Hanks was very popular.

8. Charles Lindbergh flew to Paris in the Spirit of Saint Louis in 1927.

9. The scientific name for the common grass snake is Natrix natrix.

10. I think I read that in the National Geographic magazine.

Italics and Quotation Marks

Italics and **quotation marks** are used to punctuate titles. (See *Write Source* pages 494 and 502.)

Examples

I titled my poem "Singing Seashells."

Directions — Add the correct punctuation to the titles in the following sentences. Use underlining in place of italics. The first sentence has been done for you.

1. One chapter in <u>Write Source</u> is called "One Writer's Process."

2. On page 296 there is a tall tale called Jack and the Popcorn Stalk.

3. I like the poem Toucan on page 280 in Write Source.

4. The chapter Writing Poems has a split couplet called Moira.

5. My favorite story is The Green, Howling Day on pages 89-90.

6. Owl and Highlights for Children are two magazines that publish student writing.

7. For fun, I read to my family out of my Guinness Book of World Records.

8. Our community newspaper is the Standard Press.

34

Directions Fill in each blank below with an example title. If you don't know a title for each category, look for one.

1. Title of a magazine: _____

2. Title of a magazine article: _____

3. Title of a movie: _____

4. Title of a video: _____

5. Title of a book: _____

6. Title of a poem: _____

7. Title of a TV show: _____

8. Title of a music CD: _____

The Next Step Now write sentences using the titles you wrote down. (You may use more than one title in a sentence.) Make sure to punctuate the titles correctly.

1. _____

_____

2. _____

_____

3. _____

_____

4. _____

_____

Dashes

A **dash** is used to show a sudden change in thought or direction. (See *Write Source* page 504.)

Example

Harriet the Spy—it was made into a movie—is by Louise Fitzhugh.

Directions   Each sentence below contains a sudden change in direction. Add dashes to show where each change begins and ends. The first sentence has been done for you.

1. Mildred D. Taylor—she wrote *Song of the Trees*—is my favorite author.

2. *Charlotte's Web* Charlotte is a spider is by E. B. White.

3. Molly's favorite story also about a spider is the one about Anansi.

4. *Little House on the Prairie* there was a TV show based on it is by Laura Ingalls Wilder.

5. *How to Eat Fried Worms* the whole book is as funny as the title is one of my favorites.

6. Yoshiko Uchida maybe you have read some of her books is a Japanese American.

The Next Step   Write two sentences about books, stories, or authors. Include a sudden change in direction in each sentence. Make sure to use dashes correctly.

Parentheses

Parentheses are used around words that add extra information to a sentence or make an idea clearer. (See *Write Source* page 504.)

Example

The man in the white lab coat (Dr. Zimmerman) will conduct an experiment for the class.

 **Directions** ▶ Place parentheses around the phrases below that either add information or make an idea clearer.

1   Grandpa went to grade school another name for elementary

2   school in the '50s. He remembers watching Mr. Wizard a science

3   teacher every week on TV. Mr. Wizard did some experiments that

4   explained information scientific principles in a fun way. Mr. Wizard

5   taught a lesson about vacuums not the kind that clean carpets with a

6   milk bottle, a candle, and a hard-boiled egg. Burning the candle in the

7   bottle an old-fashioned glass kind used up the air, and then the egg

8   balanced on top got pulled into the bottle. Vacuums empty spaces just

9   naturally want to be filled with something. We learned in our science

10   class that black holes outer-space vacuums pull matter into themselves

11   with great force. Besides vacuums, Grandpa learned about electricity,

12   magnets, and the effects of liquid nitrogen a very cold substance on

13   rubber bands.

Punctuation Review 1

Directions Add commas, quotation marks, and apostrophes where they are needed in the following sentences. The first sentence has been done for you.

1. Mom didn't believe me when I told her that Robby has five guinea pigs, three hamsters, three cats, two rabbits, and a goose.

2. Robby was kidding you she said. Or maybe you didnt hear what he said.

3. Being very curious my mom went over to Robbys house and she saw that I was right.

4. Five guinea pigs three hamsters three cats two rabbits and a goose! she said, shaking her head. I saw it and I still couldnt believe it!

5. Robbys mom Mrs. Davison explained that their family adopts animals that need homes.

6. The guinea pigs pen and hamsters cages are in Robbys room.

7. The cats favorite place is the kitchen.

8. The rabbits hutch is in the backyard.

9. The goose Buster lives in a big cage that Mr. Davison built.

10. Dear you know of course we cant have a zoo at our house Mom warned.

38

Add any needed punctuation to the sentence beginnings below. Then use your imagination to complete the sentences and the story.

1. Robbys guinea pigs are named _____

_____

2. His hamsters names are _____

_____

3. The cats names are _____

_____

4. The rabbits names are _____

_____

5. Busters cage door was left open one day and a goose on the loose can

_____

_____

_____

_____

_____

_____

_____

Punctuation Review 2

Directions Each sentence below needs a semicolon or colon. Add the correct punctuation mark in the correct place.

1. Yesterday, our class had Ethnic Food Day everybody brought special snacks.

2. We sampled food from four continents Asia, Africa, Europe, and North America.

3. Sue's family is from Thailand she made watermelon slushes.

4. These are the ingredients for one watermelon slush three or four ice cubes, one cup of watermelon chunks, and one or two spoonfuls of sugar.

5. First you blend the ice cubes in a blender then you add the melon and sugar.

6. Blend again until everything is mixed your tropical treat is ready!

7. You can also use any of the following fruits pineapple, oranges, lemons, or limes.

8. Vijay said kids in India love popcorn they put red pepper on it instead of salt.

9. He said that kids in Nepal eat popcorn, too they put sugar on theirs!

40

Directions ▶ Add dashes or a hyphen to each sentence below. If a word is incorrectly divided at the end of a line, correct it.

1. Nutella spread it's made with chocolate is a favorite snack in

   Europe.

2. Kids there especially in France eat Nutella chocolate sp-

   read on bread after school.

3. Brian said chocolate sandwiches sounded like a half baked idea.

4. But Chantal she's from Paris got him to try some.

5. He said it was okay, but not his all time favorite.

6. "I'll stick with all American peanut butter and jelly," he said.

7. Chantal's dad is an ex chef.

8. He made a French snack using his great grandmother's recipe.

9. There were plenty of escargots that's French for snails for every-

   one.

10. Brian he's always trying to be funny said he wouldn't eat snails,

    even if they were dipped in Nutella chocolate spread.

11. Peanut butter is a tasty, protein rich snack.

12. In Ghana that's a country in Africa people make peanut bu-

    tter soup.

Mixed Review 1

This activity uses punctuation that you've seen in previous exercises. Get ready for a challenge! It includes dashes, end punctuation, italics and underlining, hyphens, colons, quotation marks, commas, and apostrophes.

 **Directions** Some of the punctuation has been left out of the following paragraphs. The number at the end of each line tells you how many punctuation marks need to be added to that line. Add the correct punctuation. The first line has been done for you.

1   My brother—he's in sixth grade—and I never agree on   (2)

2   what videos to rent Last week, Peter that's my brothers   (3)

3   name wanted Spider Man II. I wanted Scoobey-Doo 2:   (3)

4   Monsters Unleashed. Finally, we agreed to get Beauty and   (2)

5   the Beast. We had both read the book and we wanted to see   (2)

6   if the movie was as good. What do you think we discovered   (1)

7   All the copies of course had been rented.   (2)

8   "Now what?" my brother asked   (1)

9   I guess we get our all time favorites again I said.   (4)

10   We finally left the video store with the following movies   (1)

11   Finding Nemo Star Wars: Attack of the Clones and Seabiscuit   (6)

12   When our mom saw us she asked us why we didnt get   (2)

13   something we hadnt seen before. Peter and I both said,   (1)

14   "Dont ask!"   (1)

Mixed Review 2

This activity reviews seven kinds of punctuation.

Directions ▶ Add the needed punctuation to the sentences below.

1   Although many people dont know it Washington is the fourth

2   capital of the United States Three other cities have served as

3   the nations capital Philadelphia New York and Princeton The

4   current capital is named for George Washington and he picked

5   the diamond shaped site for the 100 square mile city The White

6   House Congress and the Supreme Court are all in Washington DC

7   The White House home of the presidents family hasnt always

8   been white In 1814, British soldiers burned it the house was left

9   blackened by smoke After workers painted the house to cover the

10   smoke it was called the White House President Andrew Jackson

11   his nickname was Old Hickory added indoor plumbing

12   The White House has 132 rooms. The first floor rooms are

13   used for public events These famous rooms include the East Room

14   the Red Room the Green Room and the Blue Room Second floor

15   and third floor rooms are where the First Family lives The White

16   House has its own movie theater barbershop and dentists office

Capitalization 1

The basic rules for using **capital letters** are simple: Capitalize the first letter of a sentence and all proper nouns. Names of days, months, holidays, a team and its members, geographic places, and words used as names are all considered to be proper nouns. (See the rules on *Write Source* pages 508–514.)

Example

It was a *Saturday* baseball game in *July*.

(Capitalize the first letter of a sentence and all proper nouns.)

 **Directions** In the sentences below, find and change the words that should be capitalized. The first sentence has been done for you.

1. My uncle took my brother and me to see the ~~s~~t. ~~l~~ouis ~~c~~ardinals.
   <small>S   L   C</small>

2. The game was at busch stadium in st. louis.

3. The cardinals played the cincinnati reds.

4. My uncle said there was another game on sunday.

5. My brother said he didn't think mother would let us go; she wanted us

   to go with her to springfield, illinois.

6. But I said that maybe uncle could get mom to let us go to the game

   instead.

7. Then our uncle said he'd invite mom and dad to the game, too.

8. We all had a great time, and the cardinals won 10–7.

44

Directions ▶ Capitalize words correctly in the following sentences.

1. On the fourth of july, we watched fireworks explode over lake michigan in milwaukee, wisconsin.

2. Earlier in the week, we saw the brewers play at miller park, which is built on the site of the old milwaukee county stadium.

3. Our uncle still wanted to show us the milwaukee public museum and mitchell park horticultural conservatory.

4. We only had two days of our vacation left, thursday and friday, before we had to board a plane at general mitchell international airport and fly home to tampa, florida.

5. Next year, our relatives will visit florida in either november or december for thanksgiving or christmas.

6. We want to take them to lake okeechobee and to everglades national park.

The Next Step Write a paragraph about a game, concert, or other event you attended or would like to attend. Include as much information as you can about when and where it was, what teams or performers you saw or would like to see, and so on. Be sure to capitalize correctly.

Capitalization 2

Capitalize the names of organizations, religions, languages, nationalities, historical events and documents; official names of products; titles used with names; direction words that name parts of the country; and the titles of books, movies, and so on. (See *Write Source* pages 508–514.)

Example

The *Sierra Club* helps protect the environment.

(Capitalize the name of an organization.)

 **Directions** In each sentence below, there are words or phrases that should be capitalized. Make the needed corrections. The first sentence has been done for you.

1. The governor of Oregon, ~~s~~enator Morgan, and ~~g~~overnor Velotti gave speeches.

2. Two senators, congressman Marek, and mayor Rios held a news conference in Chicago.

3. Standing to the side were mrs. rios and her secretary, ms. shmitt.

4. Many people confuse the declaration of independence and the U.S. constitution.

5. The american red cross helps people after disasters.

6. My friend is south african; she speaks english with an accent.

7. In India, 80 percent of the people are hindu.

46

1. The action in the book *gone with the wind* takes place in the south during the civil war.

2. Two earlier wars fought within the united states' borders were the american revolutionary war and the war of 1812.

3. A movie made in the year 2000, *the patriot*, is about the revolution that took place in colonial America.

4. The main character is a hero from the french and indian war.

5. An event known as the boston tea party took place in 1773, before the revolution.

6. Many chests of tea belonging to the british east india company were dumped into boston harbor.

7. Of course, the east coast was the first area to be settled by colonists. Jamestown, virginia, was founded in 1607. Regions like the southwest, the west, and the pacific northwest were settled later.

The Next Step Write five sentences about a historical event you have studied in school. Be sure to include the full names of the people and places involved in the event. Trade papers with a partner and check each other's capitalization.

Plurals 1

There are many rules for making **plurals**. (See *Write Source* pages 516 and 518.)

Examples

cow ➜ cows
(Most nouns add an -s.)

church ➜ churches
(Nouns ending in *sh, ch, x, s,* or *z* add *es.*)

penny ➜ pennies
(Nouns ending in *y* that follows a consonant change *y* to *i* and add -es.)

Directions ➤ Write the plural form of each word listed below.

1. fox _____

2. beach _____

3. class _____

4. horse _____

5. llama _____

6. ash _____

7. address _____

8. tree _____

9. lunch _____

10. loss _____

11. spider _____

12. pony _____

13. fly _____

14. city _____

15. bush _____

16. day _____

17. eye _____

18. nest _____

19. book _____

20. boy _____

48

Examples

radio ➜ **radios**
(Nouns ending in a vowel and *o* add *-s*.)

potato ➜ **potatoes**
(Nouns with a consonant before the *o* add *-es*.)

piano ➜ **pianos**   alto ➜ **altos**   taco ➜ **tacos**
(Musical and Spanish nouns ending in *o* add *-s*.)

handful ➜ **handfuls**
(Nouns ending in *ful* add *-s*.)

reef ➜ **reefs**
(Add *-s* if a final *f* is still heard in the plural form.)

knife ➜ **knives**   hoof ➜ **hooves**
(Change *f* or *fe* to *v* and add *-es* when the plural form has a *v* sound.)

Directions ▶ **Underline the correct plural word within each set of parentheses.**

1   It was a normal day on the farm. My two aunts came from

2   the garden with *(apronsfull / apronfuls)* of ripe *(tomatos / tomatoes)*.

3   Farmers' *(wives / wifes)* are always busy. Uncle Fred was fixing the

4   shed *(rooves / roofs)*. Grandpa and my brother were spreading straw

5   for the *(calfs / calves)*. After our meal at the end of the day, which

6   included *(loaves / loafs)* of homemade bread and jam, Grandpa brought

7   out his *(banjoes / banjos)*. We had some music and *(soloes / solos)*

8   besides the sing-alongs. Finally, Uncle Fred told the stories we'd all

9   waited for—the ones about the *(rodeos / rodeoes)* he'd ridden in.

The Next Step On your own paper, write a short story (real or made-up). Use as many of the plural words on this and the previous page as you can.

Plurals 2

Making plurals isn't always as simple as adding an -s to the end of a word. Some nouns are irregular, and their spelling changes for the plural. Compound words add -s or -es to the main word. Symbols, letters, and numerals also add -s. (See *Write Source* page 518.)

Examples

two **men**

maids of honor in weddings

Directions ▶ Make all of the following words plural. The first one has been done for you.

1. woman _women_

2. child _____

3. fish _____

4. goose _____

5. cactus _____

6. ox _____

7. tooth _____

8. foot _____

9. deer _____

10. matron of honor _____

11. brother-in-law _____

12. secretary of state _____

13. sheep _____

14. mouse _____

15. house of assembly _____

16. father-in-law _____

17. chief executive officer _____

18. commander in chief _____

Directions ▶ Write the correct plural above each underlined letter or word below.

1. My dad has several degrees: two <u>B.A.</u>, two <u>M.A.</u>, and one Ph.D.

2. Ricky has a lot of <u>*and*</u>, <u>*but*</u>, and <u>*so*</u> in his paragraph.

Plural Review

 **Directions** Working in groups, think of a noun that fits each of the plural rules in your text. Write down at least one word for each rule; then write its plural form. (Important: Don't use words from the previous exercise.)

1. Singular noun: _____

   Plural noun: _____

2. Singular noun: _____

   Plural noun: _____

3. Singular noun: _____

   Plural noun: _____

4. Singular noun: _____

   Plural noun: _____

5. Singular noun: _____

   Plural noun: _____

6. Singular noun: _____

   Plural noun: _____

7. Singular noun: _____

   Plural noun: _____

8. Singular noun: _____

   Plural noun: _____

Abbreviations

An **abbreviation** is a shorter way to write a word or phrase—a shortcut! (See *Write Source* pages 520 and 522.)

Example

Dr. Wilson watches *ER* on his big *TV*.

(*Dr.* is an abbreviation for *Doctor*. *ER* is an abbreviation for *emergency room*. *TV* is an abbreviation for *television*.)

 **Find all the words that can be abbreviated and change them to their shortened form. *Hint:* You'll find 11. The first one has been done for you.**

                                    Mr.

1   Our neighbor, ~~Mister~~ Wilson, asked me to help him move his

2   television tomorrow. It's lucky I know the way to his house! I won't

3   have to use the radio detecting and ranging set I made myself. I'll take

4   my portable compact disc player along.

5   Mr. Wilson used to work for the Central Intelligence Agency in

6   Washington, District of Columbia. He's funny! His son works in a

7   hospital, so Mister Wilson calls him Doctor Wilson. But he calls me

8   Doctor Franklin, too, even though I'm only nine. Mister Wilson has

9   given me a great idea, though! I think I'll check over Doctor Doolittle,

10   the Wilsons' cat. Here, kitty, kitty!

52

Directions ▶ Match the following terms to their correct abbreviations.

____ 1. C.E.

____ 2. PO Box

____ 3. ATM

____ 4. mpg

____ 5. oz.

____ 6. p.

____ 7. a.m.

____ 8. Sr.

____ 9. FYI

____ 10. km

a. kilometer

b. for your information

c. senior

d. the Common Era

e. post office box

f. automatic teller machine

g. miles per gallon

h. ante meridiem (before noon)

i. ounce

j. page

Directions ▶ Fill in each blank with the correct abbreviation from the list.

Jr.   lb.   etc.   mph   M.D.   Mrs.   p.m.   Dr.

1   Avary Madson, _____, rushed to the hospital. He was clocked at

2   50 _____, which was too fast, against the law, unwise, _____ The officer

3   who stopped _____ Madson gave him a police escort after he heard it

4   was an emergency. At 11:59 _____, just before midnight, _____ Madson

5   gave birth to an 8-_____ baby boy, Avary Madson, _____ !

The Next Step On your own paper, write a humorous or exciting story. Use as many abbreviations as you can. Exchange stories with a partner and check to see that you've each used correct abbreviations.

Numbers

When you use **numbers** in math, you always write them as numerals. But when you use numbers in your writing, you write them as either numerals or words, depending on the rule. (See *Write Source* page 524.)

Examples

My class has *26* students in it. *Twenty* of us ride the bus.

 In the sentences below, all the numbers are written as words. Some of them should be written as numerals. Using the rules in your textbook, find the numbers that should be written as numerals and change them.

1. There are three kids in our family, ages nine, eleven, and thirteen.

2. New York City has a population of eight million eight thousand people.

3. Tokyo is even larger with eleven point eight million people!

4. Eight people got on the bus at fourteen twenty Main Street.

5. We were assigned fifteen problems on pages three-five.

6. On April seven, two thousand four, I turned nine years old.

7. Sixteen kids in our class got one hundred percent on the spelling test.

8. The family of six children had a total of eleven cavities at their last

   checkup.

9. My uncle raised nine children on a forty-acre farm in Minnesota.

10. There are more than two hundred million people in the United States.

1   In nineteen-o-nine, gold was discovered in Iditarod, Alaska.

2   Iditarod was six hundred twenty-nine trail miles west of what is now

3   Anchorage. In nineteen ten, the United States constructed a winter

4   trail through Iditarod and all the way to Nome, another mining town.

5   During the long winters, sled dogs pulled mail and supplies to the

6   towns along the trail.

7   To keep this history alive, the Iditarod Trail Sled Dog Race was

8   first held in 1967. It was a short race, covering only twenty-seven

9   miles of the one thousand one hundred fifty-mile trail. The winning

10   musher and dog team won $ twenty-five thousand. After another short

11   race in 1969, the organizers planned a nineteen seventy-three race all

12   the way to Nome. Nowadays, teams leave Anchorage at two-minute

13   intervals, beginning at ten a.m. on the first Saturday in March. Those

14   who finish the race usually reach Nome in 10 to seventeen days. The

15   1995 winner finished in 9 days, two hours, and forty-two minutes.

16   Summer hours for the Iditarod Headquarters in Wasilla, Alaska,

17   are mid-May to mid-September, 8:00 a.m. to seven p.m., seven days a

18   week. Tourists can take dog-cart rides between nine a.m. and 6:00 p.m.

Spelling Practice

Catching your spelling errors takes practice. Proofreading is the final review you give your writing before sharing your final copy. (See pages 528–535 in *Write Source*.)

 **Directions** In the following story, label the underlined words as "C" for correct, or cross out the word and write the correct spelling above. Also circle the incorrect spellings that a computer spell checker would *not* catch. The first sentence has been done for you.

1   Just a <u>few</u> blocks from our city ~~naborhood~~ *neighborhood*, a stand of   *C*

2   hardwood trees separates us from the highway. When we ride <u>our</u>

3   bikes <u>too</u> the woods, we inhale the fresh <u>heir</u> as we get closer.

4   A <u>massive</u>, old oak tree stands majestically <u>amung</u> smaller trees,

5   <u>bushs</u>, and wildflowers. Its trunk is so wide around, none of us

6   can put our arms <u>arround</u> it! Its bark forms <u>diffrent</u> patterns as

7   it crawls up the tree, and the tips of its <u>branchs</u> reach for the

8   <u>summar</u> sky. We climb this tree <u>offen</u>, feeling its strength as we

9   sit on its <u>enormus</u> limbs. On a windy day, smaller <u>branchs</u> will

10   <u>sudenly</u> <u>brake</u> off with a crack as the <u>leafs</u> rustle <u>aginst</u> one

11   another.

Spelling Strategies

Here are some ways to help you remember how to spell a word. (See *Write Source* page 528.)

Examples

Use Sayings:

PRINCIPAL - I have a **pal** in the princi**pal**.

Make Up an Acrostic (Funny Sentence):

GEOGRAPHY - Giraffes **e**at **o**ld, **g**reen **r**ice **a**nd **p**aint **h**ouses **y**ellow.

Use Familiar Words:

two ➜ **tw**in

sign ➜ **sign**ature

Directions ▶ Follow the instructions in each of the sentences below.

1. Make up a saying to help you remember how to spell the word "balloon."

   _____

   _____

   _____

2. Create an acrostic for the word "courtesy."

   _____

   _____

3. Explain why it is easy to spell "government" when you know how to spell "govern."

   _____

   _____

   _____

Spelling with Suffixes 1

If a word ends with a *silent e,* drop the *e* before adding an ending (suffix) that begins with a vowel.

Examples

use ➜ us**ing** ➜ us**able**

nine ➜ nine**ty**

(Don't drop the *e* when the suffix begins with a consonant.)

 **Directions** ➤ Add the suffixes as indicated to the following words that end in e. The first one has been done for you.

	-ing	-ment
1. advertise	*advertising*	*advertisement*
2. encourage		
3. achieve		

	-able	-ing
4. believe		
5. advise		
6. love		

	-ive	-ion
7. decorate		
8. cooperate		
9. operate		

Spelling with Suffixes 2

When a one-syllable word with a short vowel needs the ending *-ed, -er,* or *-ing,* the final consonant is usually doubled. (See *Write Source* page 528 for more information.)

Example

drop → drop**ped** → drop**per** → drop**ping**

Directions   **Complete the story by filling in each blank with the correct spelling of the word in parentheses.**

1   My friend Sal and I _____ to go fishing. She said she
     (plan + ed)

2   could catch a _____ fish than I could, and soon we were
     (big + er)

3   _____ in the backyard for worms. We _____ our
   (dig + ing)   *(grab + ed)*

4   tackle and started _____ toward the lake.
               (run + ing)

5   "Come on!" Sal yelled. "I've got to catch a _____!" We
                                         (whop + er)

6   both _____ onto the pier and found a place to fish. Sal
        (step + ed)

7   _____ as she baited her hook. Worms squirmed on our hooks,
   (hum + ed)

8   turtles were _____ nearby, and suddenly both _____
             (sun + ing)   *(bob + er + s)*

9   dunked deep.

10   "Hah!" Sal said as she was _____ the hook.
                             (set + ing)

11   "Just wait," I said, and pulled up hard. We each had a fish. Which

12   was _____ didn't matter. The fish _____ and _____.
       (big + er)   *(flip + ed)*   *(flop + ed)*

13   When we finally _____ them, we high-fived each other and
                  (net + ed)

14   _____ the fish back into the lake.
   (slip + ed)

Spelling Rules 1

Some words have letters that you do not pronounce. These are called **silent letters**. (See *Write Source* page 528.)

Examples

write	ha**l**f
foreig**n**	dou**b**t
lig**h**t	**k**now

Refer to "Improving Spelling" on *Write Source* pages 528–535. Circle the misspelled word in each sentence. Then write the correct spelling of the word on the line. The first one has been done for you.

climbs   1. Joshua's cat always (clims) into open dresser drawers.

_____   2. After Shawn rote her letter, she drew flowers around the border.

_____   3. Dad stores his ice-fishing shed on an iland all summer.

_____   4. Glenna enjoys lisening to crickets chirping at night.

_____   5. Reba knew the anser to the "Question of the Day."

_____   6. The steaming hot coco is buried in marshmallows.

_____   7. Ants scurried away with crums leftover from our picnic.

_____   8. Falling leaves, apple pies, and monarch butterflies remind me of autum.

Spelling Rules 2

To make plurals of words that end in *y*, change *y* to *i* and add *-es*.

Examples

bully ➔ bullies   country ➔ countries

toy ➔ toys   monkey ➔ monkeys

(If the word ends in a vowel plus *y*, just add *s*.)

To spell words with *i* and *e* together, remember this: "*i* before *e*, except after *c*, or when rhyming with *say*, as in *neighbor* and *weigh*."

Examples

believe   receive   sleigh

Some exceptions: either   weird   heir

(See *Write Source* page 528 for more information on these rules.)

 **Write "C" for correct if a word is spelled correctly. Otherwise, spell the word correctly.**

1. _____ pullys

2. _____ boyes

3. _____ fries

4. _____ ladys

5. _____ crys

6. _____ freight

7. _____ wieght

8. _____ joyes

9. _____ niether

10. _____ acheive

11. _____ alleys

12. _____ wayes

13. _____ beleif

14. _____ beautys

15. _____ citys

16. _____ communities

17. _____ bodyes

18. _____ freind

Spelling Review 1

You can avoid some spelling errors by learning a few basic spelling rules. (See page 528 and also review the plurals rules on pages 516 and 518 in *Write Source*.)

 **Directions**   Use the list of spelling words beginning on *Write Source* page 532. Add at least three words to each list below.

Words that end in *y* and their plurals

emergency   *emergencies*

_____   _____

_____   _____

_____   _____

Words that need their final consonants doubled when adding a suffix

getting

_____

_____

_____

_____

Words that have the vowels *i* and *e* together

receive

_____

_____

_____

_____

Words that end in silent *e* (often dropped before adding a suffix)

judgment

_____

_____

_____

_____

Spelling Review 2

Directions In the following story, label the underlined words as "C" for correct or cross out the word and write the correct spelling above.

1   This is a <u>wierd</u> story, so I <u>dout</u> that you will <u>beleive</u> it. My mom

2   was <u>beting</u> me that I <u>woud</u> <u>niether</u> dye my hair nor have the <u>curage</u> to

3   let my dad cut it. I <u>decidded</u> not to get into an <u>arguement</u> over it, and

4   just went <u>about</u> my <u>busyness</u>. Then it <u>happined</u>. My brother <u>suddenly</u>

5   <u>droped</u> two <u>pieces</u> of jelly-covered toast on my head. The <u>differnt</u> <u>jellys</u>

6   (grape and raspberry) stuck to my hair, <u>includeing</u> <u>crums</u> from the

7   toast. The gooey, <u>sticky</u> mess <u>driped</u> down my neck!

8   My dad came along and looked at me. He <u>raised</u> his eyebrows and

9   <u>plopped</u> <u>strait</u> down in his chair. "I wanted to ask you if you <u>needed</u> a

10 haircut, but I see you're <u>geting</u> a dye job first," he <u>laffed</u>.

11   Since there were no <u>artifisial</u> ingredients in the <u>jellies</u>, at least I

12 could say my hair color was <u>natchral</u>! The jelly did stain my hair for a

13 few days, and I <u>received</u> plenty of <u>admireing</u> comments.

Using the Right Word 1

Many words are commonly misused in writing. Learn to use the following words correctly in your writing. (See *Write Source* page 536.)

Examples

Wear **a** raincoat.
Bring **an** umbrella.

We were **allowed** to go outside.
Don't read **aloud** in the library.

Please **accept** this gift.
Everyone **except** Rainy was there.

I saw **a lot** (not **alot**) of pigeons in the park.

 **Directions** ▶ **For any underlined word that is incorrect, write the correct word above it. Do not change a word that is correct. The first one has been done for you.**

a lot

1   Getting angry can cause <u>alot</u> of trouble. William Kennedy learned

2   <u>a</u> lesson about this during <u>a</u> baseball game. Kennedy was pitching for

3   Brooklyn. He thought he had thrown <u>an</u> strike, but the umpire didn't

4   agree. Kennedy couldn't <u>except</u> the umpire's call. He got mad, yelled,

5   and then threw a ball at the umpire. It missed, <u>accept</u> the umpire said

6   the ball was in play, and the base runners were <u>aloud</u> to head for home

7   plate! <u>An</u> runner scored, and <u>a lot</u> of upset fans watched Brooklyn lose

8   the game. After hearing this story, my brother wondered <u>allowed</u> if

9   that's why people called Kennedy "Roaring Bill."

The Next Step **Write a sentence using each word correctly. Then trade papers with a classmate and check each other's work.**

Using the Right Word 2

Check the list of commonly misused words in your *Write Source* book (pages 536–540) to be sure you are using words correctly.

Examples

An **ant** is a tiny insect.
My **aunt** loves me.

We **ate** carrots.
Sarah is **eight** years old.

The **bare** wall needs pictures.
Here's a photo of a grizzly **bear**.

The sky is **blue**.
The wind **blew** hard.

The **brake** will stop the bike.
A short rest period is a **break**.
Be careful not to **break** the window.

We left Scruffy **by** the tree.
Let's **buy** him a chew toy.

You **may** go to the party
if you **can** find a ride.

Directions Fill in the blanks below with the correct word from those given in parentheses. (Sometimes, you may have to use a plural word.)

1. My two aunts took _____ friends and me to the zoo for my birthday.

   We _____ a picnic lunch under a shade tree. *(eight, ate)*

2. We walked _____ a pond to a _____ booth. A breeze _____

   as we waited to _____ tickets for the zoo train. *(by, buy; blew, blue)*

3. My _____ pointed to aardvarks eating _____ . *(ants, aunts)*

4. We saw a huge polar _____, covered with thick, white fur except

   for its nose and the soles of its feet, which were _____. *(bear, bare)*

5. Later, Stacy asked, "_____ we get off the train to walk around?"

   Aunt Marie answered, "I'm not sure that we _____." Then the

   engineer put the _____ on to stop at a concession stand. He said

   we could take a _____. *(break, brake; can, may)*

Using the Right Word 3

These words can be confused in your writing. (See *Write Source* pages 540–542.)

Examples

One **cent** is a penny.
Perfume has a sweet **scent**.
Mom **sent** me a valentine.

Sean **chose** Mark for the team.
He will **choose** Tina next.

Just **close** the door.
My **clothes** are dirty.

A **creak** is a squeaky sound.
Don't drink the water in the **creek**.

Oh **dear**, stop the car!
The **deer** grazed near the road.

Scorpions live in the **desert**.
The **dessert** was gooey.

Cindy wants to **dye** her hair.
We didn't want our sick canary
to **die**.

 **Directions** For any underlined word that is incorrect, write the correct word above it. Do not change a word that is correct. The first one has been done for you.

dessert

1   "What should we have for <u>desert</u>?" asked Mabel. "Yesterday we

2   <u>choose</u> fruit, but today let's <u>choose</u> frozen yogurt!" Soon I was <u>scent</u> to

3   get some frozen yogurt. The <u>cent</u> of raspberries always fills the store,

4   and the old floorboards <u>creak</u>.

5   "Hi, <u>deer</u>! What'll it be?" asked the clerk. Her <u>close</u> were clean

6   under her smudged apron. "I should <u>die</u> this apron red to match the

7   berry spills," she laughed. I ordered raspberry swirl. For a dollar and a

8   few <u>scents</u>, she gave me a single-dip cone. I remembered to <u>clothes</u> the

9   door behind me.

The Next Step Write a real or made-up story about going on a picnic. Use the following five words correctly in your story: *deer, creek, scent, dessert, clothes.*

Using the Right Word 4

Many words are easily confused in writing. Learn to use the following words correctly. (See *Write Source* pages 542 and 544.)

Examples

They **don't** like liver.
He **doesn't** like it either.

Four plus **four** is eight.
Wait here **for** a while.

Mmm, this is **good** cake.
You bake very **well**.

A **hare** looks like a rabbit.
My **hair** needs cutting.

Yes, I **heard** the bell.
The **herd** of cattle are grazing.

Come **here**, please.
Did you **hear** me?

Directions For any underlined word that is incorrect, write the correct word above. Do not change correct words. The first one has been done for you.

1   An adult male African elephant weighs over 12,000 pounds,

             four

2   more than <u>for</u> compact cars! Even a hippopotamus <u>don't</u> outweigh

3   the elephant. (A male hippo in <u>good</u> health only weighs about 8,000

4   pounds.) Because an elephant is a mammal, it has <u>hare</u> or fur. Its

5   tail serves the elephant <u>good</u> as a flyswatter. Have you ever <u>herd</u>

6   an elephant's trumpeting roar? Elephants can also make sounds so

7   low that people <u>don't</u> <u>here</u> them. And <u>hear</u> is another amazing fact:

8   Elephants many miles away actually <u>here</u> these deep tones. African

9   elephants live in groups called <u>herds</u>. Their large ears <u>doesn't</u> flap <u>for</u>

10   nothing, either. They are used <u>four</u> cooling their massive bodies. And

11   their long tusks work <u>good</u> as "shovels" for digging up roots to eat.

Using the Right Word 5

Some words are misused in writing. (See *Write Source* page 544.)

Examples

Say **hi** to Matt.
The flag flew **high**.

The show lasts an **hour**.
Come over to **our** house.

The cat licked **its** fur.
I know **it's** time to eat.

I can't untie that square **knot**.
Do **not** tie it so tight next time.

My **nose** itches!
Who **knows** the answer?

Scruffy ate the **whole** pie.
Dig a **hole** to plant the tree.

 **Directions** **For any underlined word that is incorrect, write the correct word above it. Do not change a word that is correct. The first one has been done for you.**

whole

1   The <u>hole</u> world <u>nose</u> that lightning is dangerous. When the

2   sky flashes and booms, <u>hour</u> first thought should be to take cover.

3   Lightning storms travel at about 25 miles per <u>hour</u>, so you should

4   <u>not</u> stay outside to watch the storm. Get in the house! <u>Its</u> the best

5   place to be. Back in the medieval days, people thought that ringing

6   church bells would stop lightning. Climbing into bell towers was <u>knot</u>

7   smart because lightning is attracted to <u>hi</u> places. The *Guinness Book*

8   *of Records* tells about people who have survived lightning strikes. <u>It's</u>

9   facts will amaze you!

The Next Step **Write a story about a storm you remember or heard about. Use the following six words correctly in your writing:** *high, night, whole, our, its, no.*

Using the Right Word 6

Some words sound alike or are easily confused for some other reason. Refer to *Write Source* page 546 for more information.

Examples

Come to school to learn.
Teachers teach lessons.

Vegetarians don't eat meat.
I want you to meet my friend.

I like to get cards in the mail.
The male birds have bright-colored feathers.

Dad's pants are loose.
He doesn't need to lose weight.

The maid cleaned up the kitchen.
She had made pancakes.

Directions For any underlined word that is incorrect, write the correct word above it. Do not change a word that is correct. The first one has been done for you.

teach
1   Mr. Fry wanted to learn us about an inventor. "Meat Elijah

2   McCoy," he said, holding up a picture. "The mail child of former slaves,

3   McCoy was born in 1844. He grew up in Canada, went to school in

4   Scotland, and became an engineer. He invented a system that maid it

5   possible for machines to oil themselves. That way, factories didn't loose

6   time fixing or oiling their machines. Mr. McCoy invented many things

7   that made machines work better. Today, engineers still work to improve

8   machinery—from machines that package meet in packing plants to

9   machines that sort male at the post office."

The Next Step Write sentences using each of the following words: *learn, teach, loose, lose.* Use some of the words correctly, as in "Don't lose your keys." Use other words incorrectly, as in "This skirt is too lose." Then trade papers with a partner and correct each other's work.

68

Using the Right Word 7

Some words sound alike or are confused for some other reason. Refer to *Write Source* (pages 548 and 550) for more information.

Examples

I have **one** brother.
He **won** a trophy.

Get a new **pair** of shoes.
Eat this **pear** for dessert.
Pare the apple with this knife.

The **past** is over.
He **passed** the ball to me.

Mom needs **peace** and quiet.
Have a **piece** of pie.

With no allowance, I feel **poor**.
Pour the milk.
A skin **pore** is tiny.

I am **quite** sleepy.
Please be **quiet**.
Let's **quit** raking.

 **Directions** ▶ Underline the correct choice in each set of parentheses.

1. The Olympic Games are *(quit / quiet / quite)* important to amateur athletes, so they work hard and don't *(quit / quiet / quite)*.

2. In synchronized swimming, a *(pare / pear / pair)* of swimmers perform, or *(won / one)* swimmer performs a solo.

3. As a gymnast performs, the crowd is *(quit / quite)* *(quiet / quite)*.

4. In the *(passed / past),* the torch relay was not part of the Olympics.

5. Since 1936, relay runners have *(past / passed)* the torch for each Summer Olympics from Olympia, Greece, to the site of the Games.

6. In the opening ceremony, doves are released as a symbol of *(piece / peace)*.

7. We watch the Olympics on TV and make kabobs with *(pieces / peaces)* of *(pare / pair / pear),* grapes, and cheese.

8. We *(pour / pore / poor)* cool drinks and cheer on the athletes, and for days afterward, we talk about who *(one / won)* and who lost.

Using the Right Word 8

Always check your writing to be sure you have used the right words. See *Write Source* page 552 for a list of commonly misused words.

Examples

I **read** a scary book.
Mae has **red** hair.

Let's **sit** on the porch.
Please **set** the chair there.

The **sea** is wavy today.
Do you **see** the ship?

Nan baked **some** cookies.
The **sum** of 2+2 is 4.

The dogs **seem** nervous.
Your sleeve **seam** is ripped.

Dad's **son** is my brother.
The **sun** will rise at 5:05 a.m.

A tailor can **sew** clothes.
Turn on the light **so** I can see.
I will **sow** sunflower seeds today.

 **Directions** ▶ Underline the correct word from those in parentheses.

1. While the ladies *(sit / set)* and *(so / sew / sow)* the *(seems / seams)* of the

   quilt squares, they tell stories.

2. It would *(seam / seem)* that many people are afraid of bats.

3. If you *(read / red)* about bats getting tangled in your hair, it's not true.

4. Bats are good; *(sum / some)* can eat 1,000 mosquitoes in an hour!

5. After the *(son / sun)* *(sits / sets)*, many bats come out to feed.

6. They *(see / sea)* in the dark by using built-in sonar called "echolocation."

7. Bats come in different colors, too—*(red / read)*, yellow, black, and brown.

The Next Step Write a paragraph about an interesting animal. Use the following six words correctly in your writing: *some, sun, so, seem, see, sit.*

Using the Right Word 9

Study these commonly misused words. (See *Write Source* for more information on page 554.)

Examples

Did Scruffy **steal** my cookie?
The **steel** beam is strong.

Scruffy wags his **tail**.
Grandpa told us a tall **tale**.

Look over **there**.
They're making a movie.
Don't bump **their** cameras.

I'd rather swim **than** run.
Then we'll play tag.

We paged **through** the album.
Juan **threw** a fast curveball.

The wind is **too** cold.
Come inside **to** read.
We have **two** new books.

 **Directions** Underline the correct choice within each set of parentheses.

1. For Venus flytraps, *(there / their)* diet as houseplants consists of *(too / two / to)* houseflies per month.

2. If you give Venus flytraps a bit of meat rather *(then / than)* an insect, the plants may start *(two / too / to)* die.

3. In the flytrap, *(they're / there)* are sensitive hairs on the leaves, and when an insect bends the hairs, the leaf snaps shut like a *(steal / steel)* trap.

4. *(Threw / Through)* the years, science-fiction writers have told some scary *(tails / tales)* about giant, man-eating plants.

5. Of course, these stories aren't true, but a large tropical pitcher plant may be able *(too / two / to)* trap a frog or *(too / two / to)*.

6. In the pitcher plant, an insect falls into a vase-like leaf, and *(than / then)* it cannot crawl out because the walls are *(two / too / to)* slippery.

7. If you want *(too / to / two)* grow a Venus flytrap, you can order a bulb.

8. *(Then / Than)* plant it in an old fishbowl to increase the humidity.

Using the Right Word 10

Review these commonly misused words from *Write Source* pages 554 and 556.

Examples

Hey, **wait** for me!
Check the dog's **weight**.

Don't **waste** water.
These pants are tight in the **waist**.

Do you know the **way**?
What did Scruffy **weigh**?

Dad is **weak** after being sick for a **week**.

In the story, the **witch** is banished.
Which book did you like best?

We need **wood** for a campfire.
Jack said he **would** cut some.

You're right on time!
Let me take **your** coat.

 **Cross out only the incorrect words and write the correct words above.**

1. Witch would way more on a spaceship to Mars . . . you're science

   teacher or your pet mouse? (Think about it.)

2. This weak's tongue twister: How much would wood a woodchuck chuck?

3. Do you know the rules, "Clean you're plate" and "Waist not, want not"?

4. Overdoing these rules could lead to waste and wait problems.

5. My brother felt week. After lifting waits for a weak, he had gained weight

   and was talking about football tryouts.

6. Muscles way more than fat, so someone who lifts waits wood probably

   weigh more than a person of the same size who sits around all day.

7. Check you're answer to the first question above. Your teacher and the

   the mouse would both way zero pounds without the benefit of gravity.

Using the Right Word Review

Directions ▶ Choose the correct word from each pair to fill in the blanks below.

1. Because you were sick, *(your / you're)* _____ going to have to

   make up *(your / you're)* _____ homework.

2. We walked *(threw / through)* _____ the mall, but we didn't

   (by / buy) _____ anything.

3. My hat is so *(lose / loose)* _____ , I'll probably *(lose / loose)*

   _____ it in this wind!

4. My parents parked *(there / their)* _____ car *(by / buy)* _____

   the gym.

5. Our class is going on *(its / it's)* _____ spring field trip tomorrow.

6. The flu left Dad too *(weak / week)* _____ to go to work for a

   whole *(weak / week)* _____ .

7. Terry *(threw / through)* _____ the baseball into those bushes

   over *(there / their)* _____ .

8. In an *(our / hour)* _____, *(our / hour)* _____ bus should arrive.

9. The soccer team *(one / won)* _____ *(its / it's)* _____ first game

   today.

10. *(Its / It's)* _____ getting *(to / too)* _____ dark *(to / too)* _____ see.

Directions ▶ Fill in each blank with the correct word.

1. Ms. Lee told a tall _____ about a cat with a 20-foot _____.

    (tail / tale)

2. There was no _____ my dog would let us _____ him.

    (way / weigh)

3. The wind _____ the clouds away, leaving a clear _____

    sky. *(blue / blew)*

4. The _____ of us easily _____ the large pizza. *(ate / eight)*

5. Grandpa _____ the _____ of cattle mooing. *(herd / heard)*

6. In the _____, we've _____ the bakery without stopping.

    (past / passed)

7. My _____ bought me an _____ farm. *(ant / aunt)*

8. Please do _____ untie that _____. *(not / knot)*

The Next Step On your own paper, use the word pairs below correctly in the same sentence. One has been done for you.

allowed/aloud   one/won   here/hear   for/four

We're not allowed to talk aloud in the library.

Sentence Activities

The activities in this section cover four important areas: (1) the basic parts, types, and kinds of sentences, (2) the methods for writing smooth-reading sentences; (3) common sentence errors; and (4) ways to add variety to sentences. Most activities contain a main practice part, in which you review, combine, or analyze sentences. In addition, The Next Step activities give you follow-up practice with certain skills.

Simple and Complete Subjects

The **simple subject** is the part of a sentence that is doing something. The **complete subject** is the simple subject and all the words that describe it. (See *Write Source* page 560.) *Hint:* Sometimes the simple subject stands alone.

Examples

Simple Subject: Marc skis often.

Complete Subject: Marc, who loves snow, skis often.

Directions In each sentence below, circle the simple subject. Then underline the complete subject.

1. Catherine visited a castle not far from Paris.

2. Roy, Catherine's friend, built a rocket out of cat-food cans.

3. Rocky, a raccoon, rode Roy's rocket to the moon.

4. A moon monster wearing a cowboy hat roared at Rocky.

5. The hungry monster ate Rocky's rocket.

6. Randy, the flying squirrel, flew Rocky back home.

7. Catherine invited Randy and Rocky to the castle for crêpes.

The Next Step Now, on your own paper, write three funny sentences of your own. In each sentence, circle the simple subject and underline the complete subject. Then exchange papers with a classmate and check each other's work.

Simple and Complete Predicates

The **simple predicate** (verb) is the part of a sentence that says something about the subject. The **complete predicate** is the simple predicate and all the words that describe it. (See *Write Source* page 562.)

Examples

Simple Predicate: My house has a big backyard.

Complete Predicate: My house has a big backyard.

 **Directions** In each sentence below, circle the simple predicate. Then underline the complete predicate. The first one has been done for you.

1. Doug (is) my little brother.

2. He is digging a hole in the backyard.

3. He plans to dig all the way to China.

4. He works on the hole every day.

5. Mom saw the hole last Friday.

6. She asked Doug a lot of questions.

7. He got our dad to help him on Saturday.

8. Mom laughed for a long time after that!

The Next Step Now, on your own paper, write three sentences about your own little brother or sister, or about a friend. Circle the simple predicate and underline the complete predicate in each sentence.

Compound Subjects and Predicates

You already know that every sentence needs a subject and a verb. However, a sentence may have more than one subject and more than one verb. **Compound subjects** and **compound verbs** (predicates) are explained on *Write Source* pages 560 and 562.

Example

Jake and Mitch raise and sell guppies.

Rewrite each of the following sentences two times. First change the sentence so that it has a compound subject. Then change the sentence so that it has a compound verb. Underline your subjects once and your verbs twice. The first one has been done for you.

1. Our class had a pet party.

    compound subject: Our class and Mrs. Nathan's class had a pet party.

    compound verb: Our class had a pet party and learned about animals.

2. Stacy held the gerbils.

    compound subject: _____

    _____

    compound verb: _____

    _____

80

3. Leslie baked cupcakes.

   compound subject: _____

   _____

   compound verb: _____

   _____

4. Juan brought dog biscuits and carrots.

   compound subject: _____

   _____

   compound verb: _____

   _____

The Next Step Write one sentence using a compound subject and one sentence using a compound verb. Exchange your sentences with a classmate and check each other's work.

compound subject: _____

_____

compound verb: _____

_____

Clauses

A **clause** is a group of related words that has both a subject and a predicate. An **independent clause** expresses a complete thought and can stand alone as a sentence. A **dependent clause** does not express a complete thought and cannot stand alone. (See *Write Source* page 564.)

Examples

Independent Clause: <u>Scott</u> <u>kicked</u> a goal.

Dependent Clause: After <u>Scott</u> <u>kicked</u> a goal

On the line before each clause, write "D" if it is a dependent clause and "I" if it is an independent clause. Add the correct end punctuation for each independent clause. The first one has been done for you.

_____I_____ **1.** Something is wrong with our computer.

_____ **2.** Our class is going to a concert

_____ **3.** While you are at the library

_____ **4.** Because I have a spelling test tomorrow

_____ **5.** That Jerry wrote

_____ **6.** I called Josie

_____ **7.** Since Ray was late

_____ **8.** Until I finish my homework

_____ **9.** Let's go

_____ **10.** Can you reach that shelf

_____ **11.** That Sharon bought

82

 **Directions** Each sentence below has one independent clause and one dependent clause. Underline the independent clause, and circle the dependent clause. The first one has been done for you.

1. (Before the movie started,) I got some popcorn.

2. I got a good grade because I studied last night.

3. We stayed inside until the storm passed.

4. Whatever we do, let's get something to eat soon.

5. Yesterday my next-door neighbor gave me five old records

   that he bought when he was a teenager.

6. He also gave me a phonograph, which I need to play them.

7. If the snow doesn't stop soon, we won't have school tomorrow.

8. I ride my bike to school unless it is raining.

The Next Step Complete the following sentences by adding an independent clause to each dependent clause.

1. While my parents talked to my teacher, _____

   _____

2. Because it was dark, _____

   _____

3. When the bell rang, _____

   _____

Prepositional Phrases

A **prepositional phrase** includes a preposition, the object of the preposition, and any describing words that come in between. (See *Write Source* pages 566 and 598.) The prepositional phrases below describe where the cats are located.

Examples

A cat is on top of the desk.
(This prepositional phrase includes the compound preposition *on top of*, the noun object *desk*, and the adjective *the*.)

Another cat is in the middle drawer.

The big cat is sitting by the desk.

One cat is under it.

 Write a prepositional phrase next to each balloon in this picture. Each phrase should tell where that balloon is located.

over the table

The Next Step Now write sentences using at least five of your prepositional phrases from the balloon picture on the previous page. Underline each prepositional phrase. The first sentence has been done for you.

1.   *One balloon is floating <u>above the table</u>.*

2. _____

_____

_____

3. _____

_____

_____

4. _____

_____

_____

5. _____

_____

_____

6. _____

_____

_____

Sentence Fragments 1

A **sentence fragment** is a group of words that looks like a sentence. It does not express a complete thought because important infomation is missing. (See *Write Source* page 436.)

Example

Fragment:
The Aztecs in what is now Mexico.
(A predicate is missing.)

Sentence:
The Aztecs lived in what is now Mexico.
(A predicate is added.)

> **Directions**   On each line below, put an "S" if the words that follow make a sentence. Put an "F" if they make a sentence fragment. The first one has been marked for you. (There are seven fragments.)

_____S_____ **1.** They built cities during the 1200s.

_____ **2.** Within their main city, parks and a zoo.

_____ **3.** The Aztecs used chocolate as money.

_____ **4.** Also traded with gold, copper, and cloth.

_____ **5.** The Maya in Central America.

_____ **6.** Built the tallest pyramid in the New World.

_____ **7.** A kind of picture writing called hieroglyphics.

_____ **8.** Wrote on bark paper.

_____ **9.** The Incas lived in South America in the Andes mountains.

_____ **10.** Built 12,000 miles of roads and huge buildings.

Directions

Read the paragraph below and underline the sentence fragments. The first one has been done for you.

1   The Crow and the Lakota were two powerful nations of Native

2   Americans who lived on the Great Plains during the 1800s. Both

3   groups' horses. The men developed into some of the most skilled riders

4   in the world. Having horses meant a man was wealthy. With their

5   horses hunted bison as a source of food, clothing, and shelter. The men

6   bows and arrows to kill the bison. Women found uses for every part

7   of the bison. They knew how to dry the meat to store it for winter.

8   Winters on the Great Plains long and very cold. Survival on the Great

9   Plains was challenging. The Crow and Lakota learned how to enjoy the

10 land anyway. Because these two groups lived near one another, often

11 fought against each other. Fortunately for them, battles did not last a

12 long time. Most of the time busy finding.

The Next Step Go back to the fragments on page 85 and add words to make them complete sentences. The first one has been done for you. Complete your work on your own paper.

Within their main city, the Aztecs created parks and a zoo.

Sentence Fragments 2

In this activity, you will practice correcting **sentence fragments.** (See *Write Source* page 436.)

Example

Fragment:
Living in the Arctic.
(A subject is missing.)

Sentence:
The Inuit people live in the Arctic.
(A subject is added.)

 **Directions**   On each line below, put an "S" if the words that follow make a sentence. Put an "F" if they make a sentence fragment. The first one has been marked for you. (There are seven fragments.)

_____F_____ 1. Called the Inuit "Eskimos."

_____ 2. The word "Inuit" means "the people."

_____ 3. Some Inuit used to live in igloos in the winter.

_____ 4. Igloos were made out of blocks of ice and snow.

_____ 5. Clear ice blocks for windows.

_____ 6. Others huts out of whale bones.

_____ 7. Also made one-person boats called "kayaks."

_____ 8. Larger boats called "umiaks."

_____ 9. Made sleds that were pulled by dogs.

_____ 10. The Inuit people have a proud tradition.

_____ 11. Now live in pre-built houses.

Directions

In the following paragraph, add the words from the list below to turn the fragments into complete sentences. Correct capitalization if necessary.

story	was	English	lived
changed	disagree	Eskimos	

1. For a long time, many people thought that Eskimos used

2. hundreds of words for "snow." Eskimos with a lot of snow, so the story

3. had to be true. New studies with that idea. Most people who study

4. languages now think that Eskimos have only 18 words for "snow." Has

5. about the same number. How did the get started? Some think that as

6. the story was told and retold, it. Things were added or left out. Lived

7. too far away. It impossible to easily check the truth of the story.

The Next Step For the fragments on page 87, add words to make them into complete sentences. The first one has been done for you. Complete your work on your own paper.

1. Explorers called the Inuit "Eskimos."

_____

_____

Run-On Sentences 1

A **run-on sentence** happens when two sentences are joined without punctuation or a connecting word. (See *Write Source* page 437.)

Example

Run-On Sentence:
A fish never shuts its eyes it can't even blink.

Corrected Sentence:
A fish never shuts its eyes. It can't even blink.
(End punctuation and a capital letter make two sentences.)

 **Directions** — Correct the run-on sentences below by dividing them into two sentences. Use correct capitalization and end punctuation in your new sentences. The first one has been done for you.

1. Earthworms have 10 hearts. Snails have eyes on stalks.

2. Grasshoppers can jump 30 inches that's like you jumping a football field.

3. Ants can lift 50 times their weight how much can you lift?

4. Squirrels bury more nuts than they dig up the nuts left in the ground sometimes grow into trees.

5. Birds' wings have feathers bats' wings are skin.

6. Camels drink as much as 30 gallons of water at one time no wonder they can cross deserts.

7. Kangaroo rats rarely drink water they get the water they need from the plants they eat.

90

90

90

Directions: Read the following paragraph and correct the run-on sentences. Be sure to use correct capitalization and punctuation where needed.

1   Crayfish live in streams and lakes lobsters live in the ocean.

2   Lobsters and crayfish belong to the same family of animals they are

3   not related to fish. Lobsters look like giant crayfish. Crayfish have

4   four pairs of legs and a set of pincers. If a pincer is broken off, the

5   crayfish will grow a new one the new pincer will be a lot smaller than

6   the old one. A crayfish has no bones the hard outer shell of the body

7   acts like a skeleton. The crayfish's tail flips quickly to move the animal

8   backward people are often surprised because they expect the animal to

9   move forward.

The Next Step   Write a run-on sentence about animals. Exchange papers with a classmate and correct each other's run-on sentence by dividing it into separate sentences.

Run-On Sentence

_____

_____

_____

Corrected Sentence

_____

_____

_____

Run-On Sentences 2

In this activity, you'll practice correcting **run-on sentences** by adding a comma and a coordinating conjunction. Here are some conjunctions to choose from: *and, but, so,* and *yet.* (See *Write Source* page 437.)

Example

Run-On Sentence:
Panda bears live in China they eat bamboo.

Corrected Sentence:
Panda bears live in China**,** **and** they eat bamboo.

Correct the run-on sentences below by adding a comma and a conjunction. The first one has been done for you.

1. There are eight basic kinds of bears $\overset{and}{\wedge}$ the big brown bears are

    some of the largest bears in the world.

2. Sun bears are the smallest kind of bear they weigh 60 to 100

    pounds.

3. Polar bears, a third kind, live in the Arctic they go swimming in

    very cold water.

4. Their thick fur keeps them warm their front paws work as paddles.

5. Grizzly bears, a fourth kind of bear, used to roam freely in the

    West now most of them live in national parks.

6. There are American black bears, Asiatic black bears, and

    spectacled bears don't forget the slow-moving sloth bears.

7. A bear travels over a large area during the summer in the winter it stays in a warm den.

8. Bears can outrun people only black bears regularly climb trees.

9. Some scientists say that the brown bear is the largest bear in the world others say that the polar bear is the largest.

10. Most bears eat just about anything they can survive in many different places.

11. Koala bears of Australia are not bears at all they are related to kangaroos.

12. Polar bears' main food is seal the bears have to hunt.

13. Panda bears eat bamboo they don't have to hunt in the same way.

14. Pandas can adapt to some changes the presence of people may cause starvation.

15. Bears are intelligent they learn how to get food from a campsite.

16. You should avoid feeding bears they don't become used to handouts.

17. Bears that eat handouts become dangerous they may have to be killed.

The Next Step Write a story about bears or another animal of your choice. Try to use at least two sentences that include a comma and a conjunction such *as and, but, so, or,* and *yet.*

Rambling Sentences

A **rambling sentence** happens when several sentences are connected with *and*.

Example

Rambling Sentence:

I got up in a hurry and I ate my cereal and then I got on the school bus and I saw my best friend.

Corrected Sentences:

I got up in a hurry and ate my cereal. Then I got on the school bus and saw my best friend.

 **Read the rambling sentences that follow. Correct them by dividing them into as many sentences as you think are needed. Cross out the extra *and*'s, capitalize the first letter of each sentence, and use correct end punctuation. The first line has been done for you.**

1. Misha and I went to the zoo yesterday. ~~and~~ W̲e saw polar bears, zebras, and elephants and we also saw seals and otters and then we got some juice and rested for a few minutes and finally, we saw the baby animals in the children's zoo and the little llamas were the friendliest babies.

2. My mom went to Japan on a business trip and she called me as soon as she got there and she said it was already Wednesday there even though it was only Tuesday here and I asked her how she could be in a different day and still be talking to me and she said I should ask my science teacher.

3. The edges of the Pacific Ocean have many volcanoes and earthquakes and when some of those volcanoes erupt, they can cause many problems for people who live near them and the people have to watch out for lava and ash and they have to use special construction materials to keep buildings from collapsing during an earthquake and they also have to watch for tsunamis, giant waves, that often crash onto shore after an earthquake happens or a volcano erupts.

4. A long time ago, the Algonquin people built birch bark canoes with frames made of cedar and they sewed the birch bark around the frame with spruce roots and then they sealed the canoe with pine pitch and they used a crooked knife, an axe, and an awl to do all this work and they made canoes that were about eight feet long and they also made canoes that were as long as thirty-seven feet.

The Next Step Write a short story about an unusual lunch time. Use *and*'s instead of end punctuation so that you have one long rambling sentence. Exchange papers with a classmate and correct each other's rambling sentence.

_____

_____

_____

Double Negatives

Double negatives are one kind of sentence problem. Do not use two negatives like *no, not, never,* or *none* in the same sentence.

Example

Double Negative:
My brother **hasn't** got **no** pencils.

Corrected Sentence:
My brother hasn't got any pencils.

In the following sentences, change the double negatives so that each sentence is correct. The first one has been done for you.

1. The first pencils weren't ~~no~~ pencils at all.

2. The Romans never used no wood for their writing tools because they

   used a lead rod.

3. Lead never needed no wood, but soft graphite needed a wooden holder.

4. Most pencils have erasers, but some people don't never use an eraser.

5. If your pencil lead breaks, you can't write nothing until you sharpen it.

6. Colored pencils aren't never meant for writing, but they are great for

   revising and editing.

7. The teacher hasn't given us no homework today.

8. The teacher said nobody should use no pen for drawing.

The Next Step   Use *not, no, never,* and *nothing* in a four different sentences. Do not use any double negatives.

Sentence Problems Review 1

In this review, you will practice correcting sentence errors you have learned about earlier.

Directions ▶ **Read the following sentences and make corrections where needed. If a sentence is correct, do not change it.**

1. Plastic is used for sports helmets motorcycle helmets are plastic, too.

2. Plastic is strong, and it is light and plastic can protect a football player's head.

3. Don't never use a broken or damaged helmet.

4. A plastic batting helmet has a special face guard.

5. Students who play hockey at school must wear protective helmets.

6. Schools don't buy no cheap helmets for their football teams.

7. Many skiers, bicyclists, and skateboarders now wear helmets, too.

8. Some helmets have bright colors other helmets have fancy designs.

9. The plastic in a helmet is very strong and resists breaking.

10. Helmets have vents to let heat escape and they have straps to hold the helmet in place and padding helps protect a person's head and makes the helmet fit better and many people have avoided serious injury thanks to wearing safety helmets.

11. Football rules don't allow no one to play with an unstrapped helmet.

Sentence Problems Review 2

In this activity, you will practice correcting many of the sentence errors you have learned about.

 **Directions**   The following paragraph contains sentence fragments, run-on sentences, and other problems. Make each sentence complete and correct. The first correction has been done for you.

But if you do, you are

1   You may think that dragons live only in fairy tales. ∧Wrong.

2   Really do exist. Komodo dragons aren't no little lizards they are

3   huge. They can grow to be 10 feet long and weigh as much as

4   300 pounds. Like other reptiles, lay eggs. Although they are big

5   and heavy, Komodo dragons can run very fast and these lizards

6   can catch small deer, wild pigs, and other small animals, and

7   their bite is deadly. Don't never have to worry about being bitten

8   by a Komodo dragon unless you live in Indonesia that's where the

9   dragons live. If you would like to see one up close and in person,

10   just go to Komodo Island National Park about 1,000 dragons

11   there.

Directions The paragraph below contains run-on and rambling sentences. Correct them by breaking them into shorter sentences. The first one has been done for you.

1   There are many types of lizards besides Komodo dragons.

2   Some of them live in the United States and one type of lizard

3   that lives in this country is the Gila monster it is poisonous,

4   and it grows as long as two feet. Gila monsters are slow-moving

5   lizards that live in the desert Southwest and they eat eggs, birds,

6   and rodents and they store fat in their tails so they can live for

7   months without food if they have to. The bite of a Gila monster

8   hurts, but it would not kill a person. Of course there are many

9   kinds of lizards that are harmless and some people even keep

10 lizards as pets and my friend Emily puts her iguana on a leash

11 and takes it everywhere with her. Unlike most other lizards,

12 iguanas eat plants, fruit, and flowers.

Subject-Verb Agreement 1

Subject-verb agreement basically means that if the subject of a sentence is singular, the verb must be singular, too. If the subject is plural, the verb must be plural, too. (See *Write Source* pages 419 and 438.)

Examples

Singular Subject and Verb:
Sheila has a chinchilla.

Plural Subject and Verb:
The students in our class have strange pets.

Directions   In the sentences below, cross out the incorrect verb and write the correct one on the line provided. The verb you choose should agree with the subject. The first sentence has been done for you.

1. Two students in our class ~~has~~ iguanas.   *have*

2. Jamila have a ferret.   _____

3. Ferrets is a lot like weasels.   _____

4. Jamila's ferret are named Gizmo.   _____

5. He run really fast.   _____

6. Jamila's golden retriever Sam love Gizmo.   _____

7. They takes naps together.   _____

8. Gizmo sneak up on Sam sometimes.   _____

9. Then he bite Sam's ears.   _____

10. He are just playing, though.   _____

Directions ▶ Read the paragraph below and correct the verbs so that they agree with their subjects. If they are already correct, do not change them.

wants

1   Joel ~~want~~ to buy a guitar. He knows that guitars are very

2   expensive, but he hope to find a good used one. Although he like the

3   sound of an electric guitar, he would have to buy an amp. Many rock

4   stars plays electric guitars. Joel's best friend, who has been taking

5   lessons for about two years, say Joel should buy an acoustic guitar.

6   Even if there are no electricity, he can still play and create great

7   music. If he wants, Joel can buy an electric pickup for his acoustic

8   guitar. Salespeople tells Joel that some top performers have acoustic

9   guitars. A music store only six blocks from his house have three good

10   used guitars. Joel have asked his father to help him pick out the right

11   guitar. His father plays guitar and is excited that Joel want to learn

12   how to play. Joel have saved half the cost of the guitar that he thinks

13   he will buy. If his father agree to pay the rest of the cost, Joel will

14   repay his parents.

The Next Step Write five sentences about an unusual or imaginary pet. Make sure the subjects and verbs of your sentences agree. Then trade papers with a classmate and check each other's work.

Subject-Verb Agreement 2

Subjects and verbs must "agree" in sentences that have compound subjects. (See *Write Source* page 439.) Here are two basic rules you need to know:

1. A compound subject connected by **and** needs a plural verb.

2. A compound subject connected by **or** may need a plural or a singular verb. The verb must agree with the subject that is closer to it.

Directions   Using the rules above, correct the following sentences by making the subject and verb agree. At the end of each sentence, write which rule you used. The first two have been done for you.

1. Either the cats or the dog ~~have~~ *has* to go out. *(Use rule 2.)*
   The verb agrees with dog, the closer subject.

2. Michelle and Cindy ~~is~~ *are* going to start a band. *(Use rule 1.)*

3. Either Tom or Marsha play shortstop.

4. Dan and Amy takes guitar lessons.

5. Chachi and Cindy is the best singers in our school.

6. Cindy's brothers or sister usually sing with her.

7. Charlie's brother or sisters is always yelling at him.

8. Jeff and Darla goes to California every summer.

9. Sue's brothers and cousin plays tennis.

10. Sue's brothers or cousin are coming to pick her up.

 **Directions** Carefully read the following paragraphs. Do the verbs agree with the subjects? If not, change the verbs using rule 1 or rule 2. If the verbs agree, do not change them.

1   José loves to paint, but walls or fences isn't what he paints.

2   Instead, José paints people and animals on canvas. He is taking a

3   class to learn how to paint better. He and the rest of the art students

4   is learning how to mix paint. Paper or canvas are used by most artists.

5   José's cats and dog is part of his first painting assignment. José and

6   one other student decides to share paint supplies during the course.

7   After a couple weeks of painting in the class, José discovers that

8   oil paints is his favorites. The teacher says that José and the other

9   students is doing very well. She announce an art exhibit as the final

10   project for the class. The students hang their paintings on the library

11   walls.

The Next Step Using the rules on the previous page, write two sentences that fit rule number 1 and two that fit rule number 2. Exchange papers with a classmate and check each other's subject-verb agreement.

Subject-Verb Agreement Review

This activity gives you practice with subject-verb agreement.

 **Directions** Some of the underlined verbs below do not agree with their subjects. If the verb does not agree, cross it out and write the correct verb above it. If the verb does agree, put a check mark above it. The first two have been done for you.

1   My brother and sisters ~~is~~ *are* all teenagers. I have ✓ learned from

2   them that teenagers is weird. For one thing, they does strange

3   things to their hair. You never know what my sisters or my

4   brother are going to do next. First, Kenny bleaches his hair; then

5   he shave his head. When his hair starts to grow again, he look

6   scary. Meanwhile, my sisters starts out with brown hair. They

7   looks fine. Then one day Kelly have blonde hair, and Kendra

8   have red hair. The next week, Kelly is a redhead, and Kendra

9   are a blonde. Sometimes they even add stripes—blue, yellow, or

10   red. My brother or my sisters is always in the bathroom doing

11   things to their hair. Sometimes they tries to put things on my

12   hair, and I have to scream for help. I tell my mom I are not

13   going to be a teenager. She say, "That is okay with me. Your

14   sisters and your brother is enough teenagers in one house."

In the sentences below, write the correct choice of the verbs shown in parentheses.

1. The whole class _____ to go on a field trip to Jacobsen's farm.
   (want, wants)

2. Students in the class _____ about getting too close to the animals.
   (worry, worries)

3. Janet and her two friends _____ they want to pat the horses.
   (say, says)

4. _____ the boys or the teacher going to sit close to the bus driver?
   (Is, Are)

5. The boys and the girls _____ that those in the back seats on the
   (agree, agrees)
   way to the farm will sit in the front seats on the way home.

6. The farmer or his sons _____ the gates every morning at 7:00 a.m.
   (open, opens)

7. Later in the day, the farmer's sons or his daughter _____ a calf.
   (rope, ropes)

8. During the visit, the farmer _____ a birdhouse for the students.
   (build, builds)

9. The teacher _____ Charlene and Sally to make a sign-up sheet.
   (ask, asks)

10. The two friends then _____ a colorful poster about the trip.
    (make, makes)

Combining Sentences Using Key Words

Too many short, choppy sentences make your writing . . . *choppy!* To smooth it out and make it more fun to read, combine the short sentences using a key word or a series of words. (*Write Source* page 445 tells you how.)

Example

Short Sentences:
At our school cafeteria, I like the lasagna.
I really like the burgers.
I like the fruit.

Combined Sentence:
At our school cafeteria, I like the lasagna, burgers, and fruit.

 **Combine each group of sentences to make one sentence. Use a key word or a series of words. The first one has been done for you.**

1. Our school cafeteria is huge. Our school cafeteria is crowded. Our school cafeteria is noisy.

  Our school cafeteria is huge, crowded, and noisy.

2. You always have to wait in a line. The line is long.

  _____

  _____

3. You're supposed to wait for your turn. You're supposed to wait quietly.

  _____

  _____

4. The three lunch ladies are nice. They are helpful. They are busy.

_____

_____

5. We had a special dessert. We had it yesterday. It was made with apples and cinnamon.

_____

_____

6. On Friday, we can choose a salad. We can choose pasta salad. We can choose lettuce salad. We can choose fruit salad.

_____

_____

7. The last school day before Thanksgiving, we have turkey. We also have dressing. We have pumpkin pie.

_____

_____

8. After lunch we help clean. We clean trays. We clean tables. We clean counters.

_____

_____

Combining Sentences with Phrases

There are many ways to combine sentences. (*Write Source* pages 445–446 tell more about how to combine sentences with phrases.)

Example

Two Sentences:
Jeff wants to become a professional baseball player. He is my brother's best friend.

Combined Sentence:
Jeff, my brother's best friend, wants to become a professional baseball player.

 **Practice combining sentences with prepositional phrases and appositive phrases. One example of each has been done for you. Notice how commas are used to set off appositive phrases. (See *Write Source* page 488.)**

1. Mr. Gonzalez is a baseball player. He is our next-door neighbor.

   Mr. Gonzalez, our next-door neighbor, is a baseball player.

2. He signed his name. He signed it on a baseball.

   He signed his name on a baseball.

3. Mrs. Fowler asked him for his autograph. She is my teacher.

   _____

   _____

4. He plays the outfield. He plays for the Texas Drovers.

   _____

   _____

5. He gave me two free tickets. They are for the last home game of the season. That was right after he moved in.

_____

_____

6. He told me to come to the dugout. He told me to come before the game.

_____

_____

The Next Step Write a paragraph about a favorite sport or pastime. Try to use several appositive and prepositional phrases. When you finish, circle them. Share your writing with a classmate.

_____

_____

_____

_____

_____

_____

_____

_____

_____

Sentence Combining with Compound Subjects and Predicates

You can combine sentences by using **compound subjects and predicates (verbs).** (See *Write Source* pages 434 and 560–562. Also see "Combine Sentences with Compound Subjects and Predicates" on page 447.)

Examples

Compound Subject:

Larry gave his speech today.

Maria gave her speech today.

Larry and Maria gave their speeches today.

Compound Predicate:

The teacher laughed. She dropped her book.

The teacher laughed and dropped her book.

 **Directions** Combine the pairs of sentences below using either a compound subject or a compound predicate. In parentheses, write "CS" if you used a compound subject and "CP" if you used a compound predicate. The first one has been done for you.

1. Tim knows a lot about computers. Nasim knows a lot about computers.

   Tim and Nasim know a lot about computers. (CS)

2. Linda made a bird feeder. She hung it in her backyard.

   _____

   _____

3. Tracy raked the leaves. He put them in bags.

_____

_____

4. Tron called for you. Patrick called for you, too.

_____

_____

5. My shoes got wet. My socks got wet, too.

_____

_____

6. I finished my homework. I helped Jamie with his.

_____

_____

7. We went to the library. We finished our research papers.

_____

_____

8. Diana wanted to go home. Reva wanted to go home, too.

_____

_____

The Next Step Use "school" and "library" as a compound subject in a sentence. Then write a sentence using "ran" and "jumped" as a compound predicate. Finally, write a sentence using "Jan" and "Lane" as a compound subject and using "talked" and "laughed" as a compound predicate.

Sentence Combining Review 1

It's time to review all the different ways you've learned to combine sentences.

 **Directions** ▶ **Combine each set of sentences below into a longer, smoother sentence.**

1. The ancient Greeks thought Poseidon caused earthquakes. He was their sea god. (Use an appositive phrase.)

    _____

    _____

2. The Japanese said quakes were caused by a huge catfish. It lived under the earth. (Use a subordinate clause starting with *that*.)

    _____

    _____

3. Scientists discovered the true cause of earthquakes. They discovered it recently. (Use a key word.)

    _____

    _____

4. The earth's crust moves. Land masses bump together.
    (Use *and* to make a compound sentence.)

    _____

    _____

5. This causes shaking. It causes buckling. It causes cracking.
    (Use a series of words.)

    _____

112

6. Bears can predict earthquakes. Other animals can, too.
(Use a compound subject.)

_____

_____

7. Bears usually hibernate all winter. The bears in a Japanese zoo
suddenly woke up before one earthquake.
(Make a compound sentence.)

_____

_____

8. They woke up early and began pacing. They paced around their cage.
(Use a prepositional phrase.)

_____

_____

The Next Step Write two short sentences about earthquakes. Your sentences can be serious
or silly. Trade papers with a partner and combine each other's sentences.

_____

_____

_____

_____

_____

_____

Sentence Combining Review 2

Here's your chance to show off your sentence-combining skills.

Directions   Rewrite the following paragraph. Use what you have learned about sentence combining to make it read more smoothly. The first combination has been done for you.

1   Everyone knows that the oceans provide fish. They provide

2   many other products, too. For example, oceans provide seaweed. The

3   Japanese use seaweed in cooking. The Irish use seaweed in cooking,

4   too. Seaweed is also used to make paint. It is used to make toothpaste.

5   It is even used to make ice cream. Oceans provide salt. Salt is made

6   from seawater—another name for ocean water. This is done in China.

7   Oceans also provide coral. Coral is used to make jewelry. Coral is found

8   in shallow water.

Everyone knows that the oceans provide fish, but they provide

many other products, too.

_____

_____

_____

_____

_____

_____

 **Directions** Now try it again. Combine some of the sentences to make the following paragraph read more smoothly.

1   The seas are filled with fish. They are also swimming with

2   stories. There are stories about dragons. The dragons have two

3   heads. There are tales about pirates. There are tales about sunken

4   treasure. There are tales about ghost ships. One ghost ship was

5   named the *Mary Celeste*. All its passengers disappeared at sea.

6   This happened in 1872. They were never found. Herman Melville

7   wrote a sea story. It is famous. It is about Moby Dick. Moby Dick

8   is a whale. He is huge.

_____

_____

_____

_____

_____

_____

The Next Step Choose one of the following: (1) Write a few more smooth, interesting sentences to finish the paragraph above. (2) On your own paper, tell a sea story you know, or make one up!

Kinds of Sentences

There are four kinds of sentences. **Declarative** sentences make statements. **Imperative** sentences give commands. **Exclamatory** sentences show strong emotion. **Interrogative** sentences ask questions. (See *Write Source* page 441.)

Examples

Declarative: The eel is slippery.

Imperative: Don't feed the fish.

Exclamatory: Look at that barracuda's teeth!

Interrogative: Do you think all sharks are dangerous?

 **Directions**   Write four sentences (one of each kind) about a favorite animal. Use the examples above as models.

Declarative:

_____

_____

Imperative:

_____

_____

Exclamatory:

_____

_____

Interrogative:

_____

_____

116

Directions ▶ Read each of the sentences below and tell what kind of sentence it is. The first one has been done for you.

<u>Interrogative</u>   **1.** Do all starfish have five arms?

_____   **2.** Actually, there are some that have as many as 20 arms.

_____   **3.** What is that starfish called?

_____   **4.** One name for it is the sunflower star.

_____   **5.** Look at that orange star near the shore.

_____   **6.** May I pick it up?

_____   **7.** No, do not disturb the animals in this area.

_____   **8.** Watch out for that large wave!

_____   **9.** If a seastar breaks off an arm, will the arm grow back?

_____   **10.** Starfish are able to regrow damaged arms.

_____   **11.** In fact, starfish can recover even if they are cut in two parts.

_____   **12.** I don't believe that!

_____   **13.** Well, it's true.

_____   **14.** How can a starfish do that?

_____   **15.** To be honest, no one really knows.

The Next Step Exchange sentences from the previous page with a partner. Check to see that your classmate has written an example of each kind of sentence. Then write a story about your favorite animal.

Types of Sentences

Write Source pages 442–444 explain the three types of sentences: **simple sentences**, **compound sentences**, and **complex sentences**.

Examples

Simple Sentence:
My beaded necklace broke.

Compound Sentence:
I picked up the beads, and Kelly restrung them.

Complex Sentence:
Kelly will restring the beads if I find stronger string.

 **Directions**   Next to each sentence below, write *simple, compound,* or *complex.* The first sentence has been done for you.

_____*simple*_____   **1.** Tomorrow I am going to start my book report.

_____   **2.** My best friend takes piano lessons because his parents think drums are too noisy.

_____   **3.** The gym teacher is strict, organized, and fair.

_____   **4.** My puppy has hair hanging down over her eyes, and she looks just like a dust mop.

_____   **5.** Our dog likes to eat shoes, but he won't touch my brother's smelly slippers.

_____   **6.** Tom and Mary danced around the room.

_____   **7.** The dog was friendly, playful, and smart.

The Next Step Write three sentences about gym class. One sentence should be simple, one should be complex, and one should be compound.

Directions   Change the following sentences to the type of sentence shown in parentheses. The first one has been done for you.

1. I know a lot about my state's capitol. I live near it. *(complex)*

   I know a lot about my state's capitol because I live near it.

2. I have lived in Lansing, Michigan my whole life. It is a great place to live. *(compound)*

   _____

   _____

3. The capitol is educational. The capitol is fun. *(simple)*

   _____

   _____

4. It has been restored. It has been rededicated. *(simple)*

   _____

   _____

5. The restoration was very expensive. Now the capitol is more interesting. *(compound)*

   _____

   _____

6. I go to the capitol. I look at the historical paintings in the building's dome. *(complex)*

   _____

   _____

Compound Sentences 1

You can combine sentences by making **compound sentences.** (See *Write Source* page 443.)

Example

Two Sentences:
John told us about his vacation.
It was scary.

Combined Sentence:
John told us about his vacation **, and** it was scary.

Directions   Combine each pair of sentences below into one compound sentence. Use a comma and a coordinating conjunction: *and, but, or, so, for, yet,* and *nor.*

1. John went hiking with his mother. He nearly stepped on a rattlesnake!

_____

_____

2. John knew he should back up slowly. He wanted to run.

_____

_____

3. John stayed cool. He slowly stepped away from the snake.

_____

_____

4. John says he's never going hiking again. His mom says he is kidding.

_____

_____

120

5. John's dad showed him pictures of snakes. John pointed to one of the pictures.

_____

_____

6. The snake he saw was a diamondback rattlesnake. He started to shake a little.

_____

_____

7. John's dad told him that snakes do not hunt people. Snakes do not want to bite people.

_____

_____

8. Hiking in the desert is fun. A hiker must walk carefully.

_____

_____

9. John had his camera and pack ready. He and his dad went hiking early the next day.

_____

_____

The Next Step Jot down four simple sentences about an animal. Then exchange your work with a classmate. Try combining each other's ideas into compound sentences.

Compound Sentences 2

You can practice using coordinating conjunctions to form compound sentences.

Directions   **For the sentences that follow, pick the best coordinating conjunction (*and, but, or, so, nor,* and *yet*) to complete each compound sentence. The first one has been done for you.**

1. Malcom hit the ball, _____*and*_____ it rolled into a street drain.

2. The boys looked into the drain, _____ the ball was out of reach.

3. They had to get the ball out of the drain, _____ the game was over.

4. Latrell had the longest arms, _____ he reached for the ball.

5. He couldn't grab it, _____ could he even touch it.

6. The boys looked for a stick, _____ none were long enough.

7. A policeman came by, _____ he asked them what they were doing.

8. They hoped he could help, _____ they told him what had happened.

9. The drain area was muddy, _____ he reached into the drain.

10. The policeman grabbed the ball, _____ the boys let out a cheer.

11. He gave them the baseball, _____ they thanked him.

12. The boys were ready to play again, _____ suddenly it started to rain.

Directions In the following paragraphs, join the short sentences with a conjunction from the list below. Place commas where needed and change capitalized letters. The first one has been done for you.

and   but   so   or   nor   yet

1   In the United States, there are two very popular types of fruit.

2   They are apples and oranges. Some people only like to eat apples, *but* ~~O~~ther

3   people only want oranges. Lots of apples are bright red. Some apples

4   are green. Many people who like red apples don't like green ones.

5   More than 2,500 apple varieties are grown in the United States. More

6   than 7,500 apple varieties are grown throughout the world. People can

7   limit themselves to just one kind of apple. They can eat many kinds of

8   apples. I don't like sour apples. I don't like mushy apples.

9   Many people think that all the oranges in this country are grown

10   in Florida. Oranges are also grown in California. Some oranges are

11   very easy to peel. People don't need a knife to eat them. Many oranges

12   need to be cut into sections. Then they can be eaten easily. All oranges

13   have vitamin C in them. Eating oranges is a good idea. Oranges can

14   be eaten. They can be squeezed to make juice. Doctors say that eating

15   apples and oranges is good for people. Eat an apple a day. Eat an

16   orange a day instead.

The Next Step Write four compound sentences about your favorite fruit. Use these conjunctions in your sentences: *and, but, or,* and *so.*

Complex Sentences 1

You can combine sentences to make complex sentences with one independent clause and one or more subordinate clauses. Often the subordinate clause starts with a **subordinating conjunction** (*although, because, if, since,* and so on). (See *Write Source* page 600 and "Write Complex Sentences" on *Write Source* page 444.)

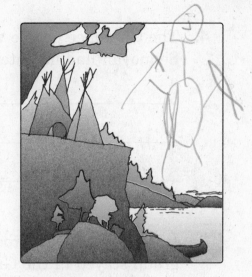

Example

Two Sentences:
Many Native American tribes consisted of 1,500 to 3,000 people.
The Cherokee numbered more than 50,000.

Combined Sentence:
Many Native American tribes consisted of only 1,500 to 3,000 people while the Cherokee nation numbered more than 50,000.

 **Directions**   Combine each pair of sentences below to make one complex sentence. Use the conjunction in parentheses.

1. The Cherokee lived in the Appalachian Mountains. The tribe was the most powerful group in the area. **(where)**

   _____

   _____

2. A Cherokee named Sequoyah wanted to contact his friends. He did not know how to write. **(although)**

   _____

   _____

3. Sequoyah formed a symbol for each Cherokee sound. He had an alphabet of 86 letters. **(until)**

   _____

   _____

4. The Cherokee people were able to write in their own language. Sequoyah had invented an alphabet meant for them. (**because**)

_____

_____

_____

5. In 1838-1839, U.S. troops moved the Cherokee to Oklahoma. A small group stayed in the Great Smoky Mountains. (**though**)

_____

_____

_____

6. The winter march was called the Trail of Tears. Many Cherokee died on that trip. (**because**)

_____

_____

The Next Step Write five sentences about a time you traveled some place near or far. Use a different subordinating conjunction from the following list in each of your sentences: *after, although, because, before, if, since, though, unless, until, when, where,* or *while.*

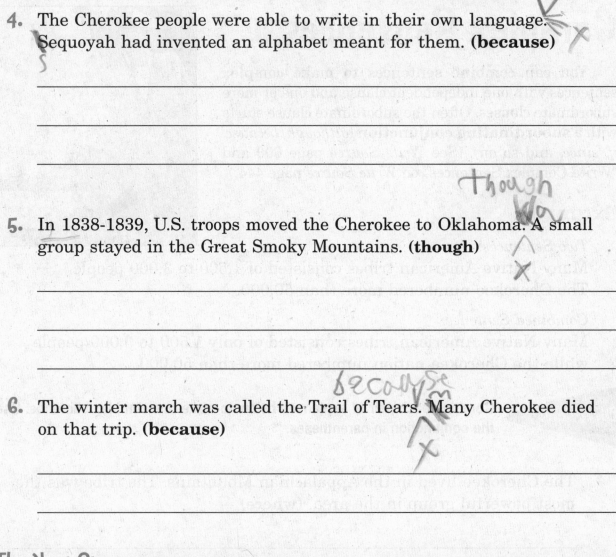

I went to wi. I Like the Long since I get to play Lots of games. Unless mom tells me to stop before I stop I beat Level. If I'm not playing between 1,2, or 3

i'm not playing at 1,2, or 3. So good bye.

I'll a different game

Complex Sentences 2

Two independent clauses can sometimes be combined with a **relative pronoun** such as *who, whose, which,* or *that.* (*Write Source* page 580 explains these special pronouns.)

Example

Two Sentences:
Creek Indians lived in the eastern woodlands. Their neighbors were the Chickasaw and Yamasee tribes.

Combined Sentence:
Creek Indians, whose neighbors were the Chickasaw and Yamasee tribes, lived in the eastern woodlands.

 **Directions**   Combine each pair of sentences below to make one complex sentence. Use the connecting word in parentheses.

1. They built more than 200 villages. Villages had 30 to 60 log houses each. **(which)**

    _____

    _____

2. The Creek lived in what is now Georgia and Alabama. They were farmers. **(who)**

    _____

    _____

3. The Creek lived in villages. The villages had central plazas. **(that)**

    _____

4. The central plaza had a rotunda. The rotunda was round and used for council meetings. **(which)**

_____

_____

5. Each town was governed by a chief. He made decisions for the people. **(who)**

_____

_____

6. The chief had an assistant. His job was to tell the people about the chief's decisions. **(whose)**

_____

_____

7. The homes of the Creek Indians were huts. The huts were covered with wood or grass. **(that)**

_____

_____

The Next Step Write a long sentence for each of the following relative pronouns: _who,_ _whose, which,_ and _that._

_____

_____

_____

_____

Expanding Sentences with Prepositional Phrases

Prepositional phrases add detail to a sentence. Use them to say more about a person, a place, a thing, or an idea. (See *Write Source* page 448.)

Example

The boy threw the rock.

The boy in the blue shirt threw the rock across the creek.

(The prepositional phrase *in the blue shirt* tells which boy threw the rock. The phrase *across the creek* tells where the boy threw the rock.)

 **In the following sentences, underline each prepositional phrase and briefly explain what each phrase tells the reader (*What kind?, Which one?, Where?, When?, How?*). The first one has been done for you.**

1. People <u>of all ages</u> love skipping rocks.

   what kind of people skip rocks
   _____

2. Flat rocks thrown fast enough can skip on the water's surface.

   _____

3. Both boys and girls shout with glee when a rock skips 20 times.

   _____

4. Some even lift their hands above their heads while they celebrate.

   _____

5. A rock skipper might not want to throw a rock after dark.

   _____

6. Rock skippers with a good arm can make 20 skips.

   _____

Directions Expand the following sentences by adding a prepositional phrase. Use the preposition shown in parentheses. Circle the prepositional phrase you add to the sentence. The first one has been done for you.

1. The window is broken. **(in)**

   The window(in my room)is broken.

   _____

2. I am going. **(to)**

   _____

3. The sign has flashing neon lights. **(above)**

   _____

4. Jenny walked. **(out of)**

   _____

5. After a long search, Mr. Gregg found his keys. **(on top of)**

   _____

   _____

6. Robert could hear his cat purring. **(inside)**

   _____

7. Please find your assigned seat. **(at)**

   _____

8. Did I see you last night? **(near)**

   _____

The Next Step Write several sentences using the prepositions *without, before, through,* and *against.*

Sentence-Variety Review

This exercise reviews different types and kinds of sentences.

 **Directions**   Identify the following sentences as "compound," "complex," or "simple." Also, list whether they are "declarative," "imperative," "interrogative," or "exclamatory." The first one has been done for you.

complex   1. Although water often looks blue, it is really colorless.
             declarative

_____   2. After you are seated, read this magazine article.
             _____

_____   3. Ricardo brought his science project into the room, and Ramon placed it near the window.
             _____

_____   4. One frog in the classroom's aquarium is green, but the other two frogs are brown with yellow streaks.
             _____

_____   5. That's a sharp knife! _____

_____   6. If you bring the right tools, you can finish the work today. _____

_____   7. You should hang your drawing on the wall, but you should not use masking tape. _____

_____   8. How many books did you read last summer?
             _____

_____   9. I found the missing football! _____

_____ 10. Don't paint the wall with that old brush. _____

Directions Combine or expand the sentences below according to the directions shown in parentheses. Make sure you include the right punctuation and change capitalization if necessary.

1. Paul carefully counted all the baseballs. Three baseballs were lost during practice. (**complex, use** *although*)

_____

_____

2. The coach thinks he saw a baseball. (**expand, use** *under*)

_____

_____

3. Waylan remembers seeing one baseball near the fence. Drake says he saw one by the dugout. (**compound, use** *while*)

_____

_____

4. Barry stopped looking. It was getting dark. (**complex, use** *because*)

_____

_____

5. Paul hopes to find the three missing baseballs. The coach will have to buy new ones. (**compound, use** *or*)

_____

_____

Language Activities

Every activity in this section includes a main practice part in which you learn about or review the different parts of speech. Most of the activities also include helpful *Write Source* references. In addition, The Next Step, which is at the end of most activities, encourages follow-up practice of certain skills.

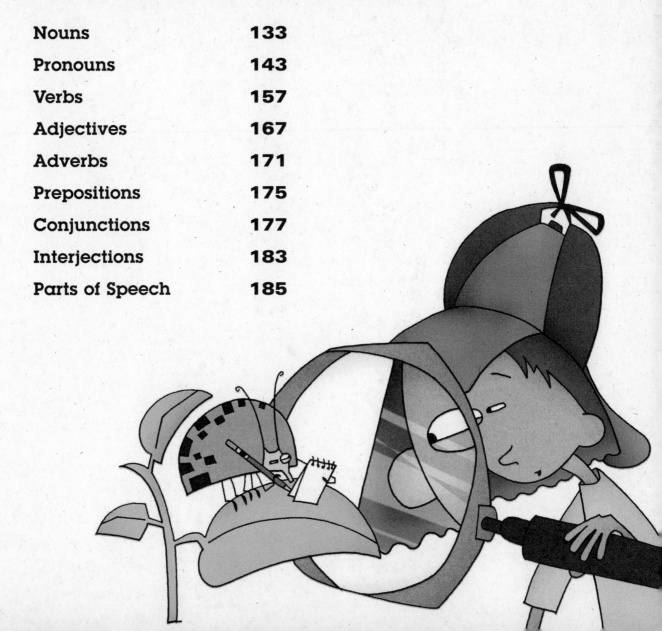

Nouns

A **noun** names a person, a place, a thing, or an idea. (See *Write Source* page 570.)

Examples

A Person: aquanaut

A Place: Mariana Trench

A Thing: bathysphere

An Idea: oceanography

 **Directions**   Circle all the nouns in the sentences below. The number after each sentence tells you how many nouns it has. The first sentence has been done for you.

1. I was so surprised you could have knocked me over with a (feather.) *(1)*

2. Don't sit there like a bump on a log. *(2)*

3. That boy is barking up the wrong tree. *(2)*

4. It's all water under the bridge. *(2)*

5. Rome wasn't built in a day. *(2)*

6. The doctors x-rayed my head and found nothing wrong. *(3)*

7. This is the greatest city in America. *(2)*

8. Forgetfulness is my biggest weakness. *(2)*

9. Don't miss tomorrow's game. *(1)*

10. Let's hope Steve gets his curveball working. *(2)*

Directions ▶ In the sentences below, circle the nouns and label each noun as "person," "place," "thing," or "idea." The first one has been done for you.

place

1. The (Atlantic Ocean) is the body of water between North America

   and Europe.

2. A scuba diver may explore ancient shipwrecks.

3. Fear keeps some people out of the water.

4. Great white sharks can be almost 30 feet long.

5. Jacques Cousteau invented the aqualung for breathing underwater.

6. Some of his friends sailed on *Calypso* with him around the world.

7. There are some dangers involved in scuba dives.

8. Deep water has a colder temperature than surface water.

9. A swimmer sometimes uses a snorkel and a mask.

10. Some people prefer a nice, warm swimming pool.

The Next Step Write four sentences about your school. Circle and identify all of the nouns.

Common and Proper Nouns

A **common noun** is the *general* name of a person, a place, a thing, or an idea. A **proper noun** is a *particular* name of a person, a place, a thing, or an idea. Remember to use capital letters for proper nouns. (See *Write Source* page 570.)

Examples

Common Nouns: man, woman

Proper Nouns: Mr. Thun, Ms. Felipe

 **Directions**   Write a common noun to go with each proper noun. Then write a proper noun to go with each common noun.

Proper Nouns	Common Nouns
1. Milwaukee	_____
2. Florida	_____
3. Pacific	_____
4. Sunday	_____
5. October	_____
6. _____	boy
7. _____	river
8. _____	team
9. _____	athlete
10. _____	school

Concrete and Abstract Nouns

Concrete nouns name things that can be touched or seen. **Abstract nouns** name things that cannot be touched or seen. (See *Write Source* page 570.)

Examples

Concrete Nouns: shoe, building, sky, Ohio

Abstract Nouns: mystery, laziness, fear

 **Directions** Sort the nouns below into two groups: concrete and abstract nouns. Write each noun in the correct column.

tractor	idea	supermarket	sun
students	strength	hope	sadness
zoo	health	thought	lawn

Concrete Nouns	**Abstract Nouns**
_____	_____
_____	_____
_____	_____
_____	_____
_____	_____
_____	_____

The Next Step Now think of three more nouns to add to each column. If you need ideas, look around you! Things you can see are concrete nouns. Moods, feelings, ideas, and so on, are abstract nouns.

Compound Nouns

Two or more words make up a **compound noun**.
Compound nouns can add interest to your writing.

Examples

flashlight	*(written as one word)*
picture tube	*(written as two words)*
sister-in-law	*(written with hyphens)*

 Choose from the list of compound nouns below to replace the underlined noun in each sentence below. The first one has been done for you.

rainbow	firefighter	president-elect
house cat	forklift	fullback
blue jeans	babysitter	fish fry

   firefighter

1. The ~~man~~ sprayed water on the burning building.

2. The warehouse worker used a <u>machine</u> to move the heavy crate.

3. Our <u>runner</u> carried the ball over the goal line for our first touchdown.

4. I saw their friendly <u>animal</u> curled up in a sunny spot.

5. Randy likes his comfortable <u>pants</u>.

6. Mom and Dad have called a <u>person</u> to stay with my little sister tonight.

7. The <u>politician</u> moves into the White House in January.

8. Bill likes the trout served at the annual <u>picnic</u>.

9. After the rain, Jeff looked for the <u>sight</u> in the sky.

The Next Step Look in a dictionary for three other compound nouns. Write a sentence for each noun.

Number and Gender of Nouns

A noun that names only one person, place, thing, or idea is singular. If it names more than one, it is plural. A noun is feminine if it refers to a female and masculine if it refers to a male. A neuter noun refers to an object neither male nor female. An indefinite noun could be either male or female. (See *Write Source* page 572.)

Examples

	Number		*Gender*	
Singular Nouns:	shoe, student	*Masculine:*	boy, son, nephew, bull
Plural Nouns:	shoes, students	*Feminine:*	girl, daughter, niece, cow
		Neuter:	nail, pencil, paper, shoe
		Indefinite:	child, parent, student, deer

Directions ▶ Identify the following nouns. The first one has been done for you.

<u>singular, neuter</u> 1. car

_____ 2. house

_____ 3. librarian

_____ 4. nephew

_____ 5. birds

_____ 6. aunt

_____ 7. bucket

_____ 8. scouts

_____ 9. coyotes

_____ 10. men

_____ 11. sister

_____ 12. hen

_____ 13. books

_____ 14. daughter

_____ 15. ladies

_____ 16. uncle

_____ 17. cow

_____ 18. rock

_____ 19. bee

_____ 20. actresses

The Next Step Choose four nouns from the list (two plural and two singular). Write a sentence with each word.

Uses of Nouns 1

Directions: In the following sentences, underline the subject noun and circle the predicate noun. Some sentences may have both a subject noun and a predicate noun. The first one has been done for you. (See *Write Source* page 574.)

1. <u>Starlings</u> are not native (birds) to the United States.

2. More than 100 years ago, a group of people brought starlings from England.

3. Many people enjoyed the metallic-colored birds.

4. Those bird lovers were surprised that starlings multiplied so quickly.

5. Aggressive starlings often drive away other birds.

6. Today many say, "These birds are pests."

7. The English sparrow is an import.

8. This plain brown bird can be found throughout the United States.

9. English sparrows are another problem.

10. The bird's nest is a messy place.

11. An English sparrow isn't aggressive.

12. Still, a flock of these sparrows often crowd out other birds.

13. Perhaps people should not import foreign birds and animals.

Uses of Nouns 2

Possessive nouns show ownership. (Check *Write Source* page 574 for an explanation of possessives.) Add an *-'s* for most singular nouns and an apostrophe after the *s* for most plurals. Some plurals need an *-'s*.

Examples

The girl's lunch was left on the bus. *("girl," a singular noun)*

The girls' picnic was delayed by rain. *("girls," a plural noun)*

The men's volleyball tournament is next week. *("men," a plural noun)*

 **Directions** **Fill each blank in the following sentences with the correct possessive form of the noun shown in parentheses. The first one has been done for you.**

1. A _____tree's_____ leaves release oxygen into the air. *(tree)*

2. The class spent an hour looking for _____ book. *(Dan)*

3. This is the last game for the _____ soccer team. *(boys)*

4. Did you find our _____ collar in the park? *(dog)*

5. The _____ mother will pick them up at noon. *(children)*

6. I didn't like that _____ cover. *(book)*

7. The _____ winds grew stronger every hour. *(hurricane)*

8. In our solar system, none of the _____ orbits are the same. *(planets)*

The Next Step Rewrite one of the above sentences so that the singular possessive noun is plural. Rewrite one so that the plural possessive noun is singular. Change words as needed.

Example: (Sentence 1) Trees' leaves release oxygen into the air.

Nouns as Objects 1

When you think of nouns, you probably think of them as the subjects of sentences. But nouns may also be used as **objects**. In the two sentences below, *dog* and *street* are objects. (*Write Source* page 574 explains nouns used as objects.)

Examples

The <u>cat</u> <u>chased</u> the *dog*.

(The word *dog* is a direct object.)

The <u>ball</u> <u>rolled</u> into the *street*.

(The word *street* is the object of the preposition *into*.)

 **Directions**   Each sentence below has at least one noun used as an object. Underline and label each object: direct object, indirect object, or object of preposition. The first one has been done for you.

       indirect object   *direct object*

1. The teacher gave <u>Julie</u> a <u>pencil</u>.

2. Mom parked behind the school.

3. Joey called the police.

4. We built a playhouse in our backyard.

5. Mom painted our house.

6. Last night, I read Brad a story.

7. Rene gave Michael a cookie.

8. Darla sent the teacher a valentine.

9. Gerardo gave a speech to our class.

Nouns as Objects 2

This page gives you more practice recognizing objects.

Directions In the paragraph below, circle the indirect objects, underline the direct objects, and underline the objects of prepositions twice. The first sentence has been done for you. (See *Write Source* page 574.)

1   Mosquitoes bother people in the summer. These insects bite

2   people more often during hot, muggy weather. Mosquitoes can

3   make an animal's life miserable. Some people swat the mosquitoes.

4   Sometimes mosquito bites aren't noticed. Later, those bites cause

5   the skin to swell. Then people may scratch the itchy bumps.

6   Scratched bumps only feel itchier. A mosquito bite can give an

7   allergic person a huge bump. On hot nights, a mosquito's noisy

8   wings can even keep adults awake. Most mosquito bites don't

9   cause trouble. Some mosquitoes can give people diseases. Parents

10   can buy insect sprays and creams for the whole family. Adults

11   give children mosquito repellant. Some of these products even

12   keep mosquitoes off the skin. Swarms of insects can ruin a nice

13   summer day.

Number of a Pronoun 1

A **pronoun** can be either singular or plural. (See *Write Source* page 576.)

Examples

Singular

Bob went to the store. | He went to the store.

(The singular pronoun *He* replaces the
singular noun *Bob*.)

Plural

The girls are hungry. | They are hungry.

(The plural pronoun *They* replaces the plural noun *girls*.)

Directions ▶ Label the underlined pronouns in the sentences below with "S" for singular or "P" for plural. Draw an arrow to the noun the pronoun replaces. The first one has been done for you.

1. Sheila looked for the blue hat, but she could not find it.

2. The wind was strong, and it was cold.

3. Sheila's brother, Dave, gave her a hat.

4. Although Sheila and Dave were cold, they kept walking.

5. Mrs. Smith said to Sheila and Dave, "You look cold."

6. Mrs. Smith decided she would give the two walkers some hot cider.

7. Sheila and Dave said to Mrs. Smith, "Thank you for the hot cider."

8. Both Sheila and Dave said they were glad to get warm again.

Number of a Pronoun 2

Directions Read the following paragraphs and replace the underlined words with the correct pronouns. The first one has been done for you.

1   My dad thought I would like a model spaceship for my

          he   it

2   birthday, so ~~Dad~~ bought a space shuttle. The shuttle was made

3   of plastic, but some parts were metal. I was excited because the

4   model was so detailed. Of course, my dad wanted to help me, so

     we

5   ~~Dad and I~~ worked together on the model. Mom and my sister

                                   they

6   liked watching us work, so ~~Mom and my sister~~ would check on

    us

7   ~~Dad and me~~ sometimes. My best friend, Joe, stopped by to help,

                we

8   too. ~~My dad, Joe, and I~~ each worked on different parts of the

9   shuttle. Then, we assembled the three parts. Once the whole

                            it

10   model was together, we set the ~~model~~ aside to let the glue dry.

11   I talked to the man who owns the hobby shop, and

    he — owner

    ~~the hobby shop owner~~ told me to use spray enamel. The hobby

    e

    ~~shop owner~~ said the spray would look better than painting by

14   and. We decided to paint the shuttle in the garage. Joe said

               him   you

15   was time for ~~Joe~~ to go home. Dad said to Joe, "~~Joe,~~ be sure

                                             he

16   t me see the model when we're done." Joe promised that ~~Joe~~

17   wo

Subject and Object Pronouns 1

A **pronoun** is a word used in place of a noun. A **subject pronoun** is used as the subject of a sentence. An **object pronoun** is used after an action verb or in a prepositional phrase. (See *Write Source* page 578.)

Examples

Subject Pronoun: We got lost.

Object Pronoun: Mom and Dad found us.

 **Directions**   Each sentence below contains a subject pronoun, an object pronoun, or both. Underline each pronoun. Write "S" above each subject pronoun and "O" above each object pronoun. The first sentence has been done for you.

1.   *S*   *O*
   We found them in the library.

2. I left it at school.

3. We helped her find the books.

4. She needed them.

5. After dessert, he read me a story.

6. You saw us at the mall.

7. He got a new sweater.

8. It fits him.

9. Yesterday, Paulo wrote me a note.

10. The teacher saw it.

148

Directions	Cross out the complete subject in each sentence below. Replace the subject with the correct subject pronoun: *he, she, it,* or *they.* The first one has been done for you.

1. ~~Philip~~ *He* likes bananas.

2. Jessica brought the cake.

3. The weather is too cold for Harry.

4. Tim and Charlie know Michelle.

5. Last night, my parents met my teacher and her husband.

6. The house belongs to Ms. Rojas.

7. After school, Jeff walked home with Sue.

8. The cat belongs to Juanita.

9. Elena found the book for Jose.

10. Mr. Montoya listened to the band students practice.

11. The close game got the fans excited.

12. Erika and Laura wrapped the present.

13. Michelle forgot to call her parents.

14. John ate the hot fudge sundae.

15. Six students helped decorate the stage.

The Next Step Now cross out each noun or noun phrase in the above sentence and write the correct object pronoun (*him, her, it,* or *them*) above it.

Subject and Object Pronouns 2

A **subject pronoun** is used as the subject of a sentence. An **object pronoun** is used after an action verb or in a prepositional phrase. A **possessive pronoun** shows ownership. (To learn more about each of these pronouns, creafully read the sample sentences and the information about personal pronouns on *Write Source* page 578.)

 **Directions** Circle the pronouns in the following sentences. Label the pronouns with "S" for subject, "O" for object, or "P" for possessive. Then go back and mark "Si" for singular or "Pl" for plural. The first one has been done for you.

     S Si   P Si

1. (He) walked with (his) dog for two hours.

2. The dog tried to run, but Jeff stopped it with the leash.

3. Then, Jeff's friends asked him to go to a movie with them.

4. They went to see the newest movie at the theater.

5. They paid for their tickets and walked toward the popcorn machine.

6. A man stopped them and said, "Show me your tickets, please."

7. Nancy used some of her money to buy gum.

8. She joined the rest of the group just before the movie got started.

9. She almost missed its opening scene.

10. Jeff whispered, "Why were you so late?"

11. "I couldn't find the flavor of gum that I like," she answered.

The Next Step Write a paragraph about something your school is proud of. Trade paragraphs with a classmate and circle all of your partner's pronouns. Then put each pronoun into the correct box below. Return the papers to each other and check each other's work.

_____

_____

_____

_____

_____

_____

Subject Pronouns

Singular	
Plural	

Object Pronouns

Singular	
Plural	

Possessive Pronouns

Singular	
Plural	

Possessive Pronouns

A **possessive pronoun** shows ownership. (See *Write Source* page 578.)

Examples

We wrote our poems on the board.
Mine was the shortest.
Yours was the funniest.

 **Directions** ▶ Underline the possessive pronouns in the following sentences. The first sentence has been done for you.

1. Our teacher read my poem.

2. The fifth graders had their field trip today.

3. The fourth grade has its field trip next week.

4. Which softball is ours, and which is theirs?

5. Did you bring your glove?

6. No, but Buddy brought his.

7. He brought his bats, too.

8. My brother is watching our jackets for us.

9. Is that my glass, or yours?

10. That's her glass; this one is yours.

11. I thought the other one was hers!

12. The one that's full is mine.

The Next Step Replace each underlined word or phrase below with a possessive pronoun. The first one has been done for you.

1   One the way to school, Jeremy dropped *his* Jeremy's backpack in

2   a big puddle of slush. All of Jeremy's books, papers, markers, and

3   everything else got soaked. When the teacher collected homework,

4   Jeremy handed Jeremy's homework in—still dripping! When

5   Jeremy needed a pen, he asked Alicia if he could borrow Alicia's

6   pen. Of course, he needed paper, too, so he asked Mark for some

7   of Mark's paper. When he needed a dry math book, he asked me

8   if he could share my math book. At lunch, Jeremy needed dry

9   food! Hannah and Todd let Jeremy share Hannah's and Todd's

10   sandwiches. Tina and I told Jeremy that if he wanted some raw

11   carrots, he could have our raw carrots.

12   Jeremy said, "Thanks, Jim, but I'd rather eat Jeremy's wet

13   cookies than Tina's and Jim's dry carrots."

14   Tina gave some of Tina's dessert to Jeremy. I gave him

15   a banana and said, "Sorry, buddy, but this brownie is all my

16   brownie!"

Indefinite Pronouns

An **indefinite pronoun** does not name the word it replaces. (See the bottom of *Write Source* page 580 for a list of indefinite pronouns.)

Examples

Several forgot their lunches.

Each of them bought a snack in the cafeteria.

 **Directions** Underline the idefinite pronouns in the following sentences. (Some sentences have more than one indefinite pronoun.)

1. Someone left all of these books here.

2. Some of us have finished our projects.

3. Most of us did all of our homework.

4. Everybody is going to the library.

5. In the end, everything turned out fine.

6. Both of my brothers are older than I am.

7. None of us remembered to bring anything to drink.

8. Each of us was supposed to bring something.

The Next Step An indefinite pronoun is a bit mysterious; it does not name the word it replaces. That means that indefinite pronouns are right at home in a mystery story! Write five sentences that sound as if they were taken from a mystery story. Use at least one indefinite pronoun in each sentence. One has been done for you.

1. *Suddenly, everyone was silent.*

Demonstrative Pronouns

A **demonstrative pronoun** identifies a noun without naming it. The demonstrative pronouns are *this, that, these,* and *those*. *This* and *that* are singular. *These* and *those* are plural. *This* and *these* often point out something close or something new. *That* and *those* point out something far away or something older.

Examples

Have you seen Ramos' red pen? **This** must be it.

 **Directions** Fill in the blanks with "this," "that," "these," or "those" to complete the sentences below. The first one has been done for you.

1. Are they still playing the game? Yes, ___*this*___ is going to be a long one.

2. Look at Jorge's model car. He bought _____ yesterday.

3. I noticed the mess in the kitchen. Who did _____?

4. I tried on the wraparound glasses and said, "_____ are some of the strangest-looking sunglasses I have ever seen."

5. Hank held up two blue hats and asked, "Are _____ for sale?"

6. What do you think of the painted carving on the table by the door?

_____ is a very pleasing art project.

7. Talk to the players at the side of the field and tell _____ without helmets that they can't play.

8. Go look at Room 22. _____ is the way to paint the walls in Room 201.

9. Mr. Thompson held up Mark's paper and said, "_____ is well done."

The Next Step Write four sentences. Use one of the demonstrative pronouns in each one.

Pronoun-Antecedent Agreement

The pronouns in your sentences must agree with their antecedents. An **antecedent** is the name for the noun that a pronoun replaces. (See *Write Source* page 414.)

Examples

Rod's sister lost her sunglasses at the beach.
(The pronoun *her* and the word it replaces, *sister,* are both singular, so they agree.)

Angie *and* Julie go body surfing whenever they can.
(The pronoun *they* and the words it replaces, *Angie and Julie,* are both plural, so they agree.)

 **Directions**   Circle the pronouns in each of the following sentences. Draw an arrow to each pronoun's antecedent. If a pronoun does not agree with this antecedent, cross it out and write the correct pronoun above it. The first one has been done for you.

1. Rod and Angie got up early so ~~she~~ *they* could go on the tide-pool walk.

2. The naturalist told the group of early-morning hikers to follow them.

3. People wore rain gear because they were told to expect rain on the

    Olympic coast.

4. As the sun rose over the Olympic Mountains, they created a foggy,

    golden glow.

5. Rod slipped on the tide-pool rocks that had seaweed growing on it.

6. Tentacles coming from the sea anemones made it look like flowers

    to Angie.

7. One deep-orange starfish lifted an arm as it moved across a rock in

   slow motion.

8. Empty sea urchin shells were scattered about where seagulls left them.

9. The yellow sea slugs crossing the pool looked like it needed a rest.

10. Angie liked barnacles that they thought looked like jumping jacks.

11. As the tide started coming in, Rod called for Angie to wait for him.

12. Then the tide pools disappeared; they will reappear at the next low tide.

The Next Step Write two pairs of sentences. In the first sentence, use a noun. In the second sentence of each pair, use a pronoun that agrees with the antecedent in your first sentence.

1. _____

   _____

2. _____

   _____

1. _____

   _____

2. _____

   _____

Types of Verbs 1

There are three types of **verbs**. (See *Write Source* page 582.) **Action verbs** tell what the subject is doing. **Linking verbs** link a subject to a noun or an adjective. **Helping verbs** help state an action or show time.

Examples

Action Verbs: ran, jumped

Linking Verbs: was, seemed

Helping Verbs: has been, will

Directions   Write down as many examples of each type of verb as you can in 5 minutes! When your time is up, use the explanations in *Write Source* to check your verbs.

Action Verbs	Linking Verbs	Helping Verbs
_____	_____	_____
_____	_____	_____
_____	_____	_____
_____	_____	_____
_____	_____	_____
_____	_____	_____
_____	_____	_____

The Next Step   Write a story about preparing and eating your favorite food. Underline and label the verbs in your story: "A" (action), "L" (linking), or "H" (helping). Share your work with a classmate.

Types of Verbs 2

There are three types of verbs: action verbs, linking verbs, and helping verbs. (They're explained on *Write Source* page 582.)

Examples

Action Verbs: watch, swam

Linking Verbs: is, appear

Helping Verbs: are, will

 **Directions** ▶ Label the underlined verbs in the sotry below as *action, linking,* or *helping.* The first two have been done for you.

            action   *helping*

1   "<u>Get</u> down, Antonio. They <u>will</u> <u>see</u> you. <u>Get</u> down."

2   Everything <u>was</u> <u>happening</u> so fast. Captain Magellan <u>was</u>

3   dead, the crew <u>had</u> <u>scattered</u> into the woods, and now we <u>were</u>

4   under attack.

5   "Juan," <u>whispered</u> Antonio. "Since the captain <u>is</u> dead, you

6   <u>are</u> now in charge. You <u>must</u> <u>get</u> us out of here."

7   Yes, Antonio <u>was</u> right. I, Juan Sebastian del Cano, <u>was</u> in

8   charge. But <u>get</u> us out of here? How?

9   There <u>was</u> no chance that we <u>would</u> <u>survive</u> if we <u>stayed</u>

10   on the ship. Escaping, as the crew <u>had</u> <u>done</u>, <u>was</u> our only hope.

11   "Antonio," I <u>said</u>, "we <u>will</u> <u>swim</u> for it."

The Next Step Continue the story. What will happen? Afterward, underline and label the verbs: "A" for action, "L" for linking, or "H" for helping. Share your work with a classmate.

Simple Verb Tenses

Verb tenses tell the time of a verb. (See *Write Source* page 584.) The **present tense** of a verb describes something that is happening now or something that happens regularly. The **past tense** of a verb describes something that happened in the past. The **future tense** of a verb describes something that will happen in the future.

Examples

Present Tense: The bear likes the sandwich.

Past Tense: The bear liked the sandwich.

Future Tense: The bear will like the sandwich.

 Circle the present tense verb in each sentence below. Then, on the lines after each sentence, write the verb in the past tense and the future tense. The first sentence has been done for you.

	Past Tense	Future Tense
1. I (play) my stereo at top volume.	played	will play
2. I dance along to the music.		
3. No one likes the sound.		
4. The stereo blasts out music.		
5. My brother covers his ears.		
6. My mother rolls her eyes.		
7. My father laughs.		
8. Our dog Elvis howls.		
9. Our cat crawls under the chair.		

160

The Next Step List three verbs below. (You can pick three from the list on page 588 of your *Write Source*, or you can use any other verbs.) Have a classmate do the same thing; then trade lists. For each of the three verbs you receive, write three sentences. Use the *present tense* of the verb in one sentence, the *past tense* in another sentence, and the *future tense* in your last sentence.

Three Verbs:

1. _____

2. _____

3. _____

Present Tense Sentences:

1. _____

2. _____

3. _____

Past Tense Sentences:

1. _____

2. _____

3. _____

Future Tense Sentences:

1. _____

2. _____

3. _____

Singular and Plural Verbs 1

Use a **singular verb** when the subject in a sentence is singular. Use a **plural verb** when the subject is plural. (See *Write Source* page 586.)

Examples

Singular Verbs: talks, gives, clucks

Plural Verbs: talk, give, cluck

Directions Give a name to each of the children below. Then write a sentence about each of them, using one of these singular verbs: *looks, wishes, waits, hopes, stares, listens, wonders, tries, keeps, sees,* and *smiles.* The first one has been done for you.

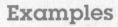

1. Marty stares at the hamster in the cage.

2. _____

3. _____

4. _____

5. _____

Marty

Singular and Plural Verbs 2

Directions   Check the verbs in the following sentences. If a verb is correct, underline it. If the verb is not correct, draw a line through it and write the correct form above it. The first one has been done for you.

1. Wylan ~~kick~~ *kicks* the ball more than 30 yards.

2. These four boys run on the same relay team.

3. They practices twice a day.

4. Ms. Fry still coach the girls' softball team.

5. Is you happy about the color of the new uniforms?

6. The team's catcher want to buy a hamburger before the game.

7. Who waters the football field in the summer?

8. A gymnast put chalk on his or her hands.

9. Fifteen players runs laps every day.

10. Coach Fry show the team how to catch a fly ball.

The Next Step   Write three sentences with the word *children* as the subject. Use one of these plural verbs in each of your sentences: *wonder, hope,* and *see.*

Irregular Verbs 1

To make most verbs past tense, you simply add -*ed* to the end. Easy. But then there are **irregular verbs**. They're called irregular because you don't make them past tense in the regular way. (For a list of irregular verbs, see *Write Source* page 588.)

Examples

Irregular Verbs: ride, rode, ridden
run, ran, run
set, set, set

Directions   Study the chart of irregular verbs on page 588. Then close your book and fill in the missing words in the chart below.

present tense	past tense	past participle
1. break		(have) broken
2. bring		
3. come	*came*	
4. drink		(have) drunk
5. know	*knew*	
6. lead		
7. shake		(have) shaken
8. sing		(have) sung
9. speak	*spoke*	
10. take		

Irregular Verbs 2

This exercise gives you practice using **irregular verbs**. (Before you begin, review the chart of irregular verbs on *Write Source* page 588.)

Examples

Irregular Verbs:

see	saw	seen
sit	sat	sat
burst	burst	burst

 **In each sentence below, fill in the blank with the correct form of the verb that appears in parentheses. Try this without looking at your handbook. The first sentence has been done for you.**

1. The rain _____ *froze* _____ and made the streets slick. (*freeze*)

2. Our cat's water was _____ , too. (*freeze*)

3. My uncle _____ me to a museum last week. (*take*)

4. He has _____ me to a lot of fun places. (*take*)

5. I _____ up at 7:00 a.m. yesterday. (*wake*)

6. I _____ my bike to my cousin's house. (*ride*)

7. I had never _____ there before. (*ride*)

8. Misha was _____ by a spider. (*bite*)

9. The spider _____ him on the foot. (*bite*)

10. His neighbor _____ over to look at it. (*come*)

11. Misha's mom _____ to the doctor. (*speak*)

Irregular Verbs Review 1

This activity gives you more practice with irregular verbs.

 **Directions** To practice using irregular verbs, change the underlined verbs to the past tense. The first sentence has been done for you.

rang
1   The doorbell ~~rings~~. I wake up. It is Saturday morning, and

2   the snow is coming down hard. My uncle stands outside our door

3   with a huge package, taller than I am. He brings the package

4   inside. A freezing wind blows in. With a wink and a smile, he

5   says the present is for me. It isn't my birthday or anything. He

6   sets it in the hallway. "Don't open it yet," he says. "What's for

7   breakfast?" I eat in a hurry. My uncle drinks coffee and talks

8   to my mom. I steal glances at the package. I fight the urge to

9   run to the hallway and open it. Finally my uncle says, "Well, I

10 guess it's time!" I run to the hallway. I shake the box—it is not

11 heavy at all for such a big box. I lay it on its side. I tear off the

12 wrapping paper. At the bottom of the box, something shines like

13 silver . . . silver with a long wooden handle. It is a snow shovel!

14 My uncle bursts out laughing. "Let it snow, let it snow, let it

15 snow!" he sings. I begin to plan my revenge, but then my uncle

16 makes it up to me: He takes me to the movies.

Irregular Verbs Review 2

Directions ▶ Check the sentences below to make sure the irregular verbs are spelled correctly. Circle the correct ones. Cross out each incorrect verb and write the correct form above it.

1. Yesterday, Jane bited into an apple and breaked a tooth.

2. The cell phone rang five times before someone answered it.

3. Janis weared a new pair of shoes for the field trip.

4. The team swam 15 laps last Thursday.

5. Susan knowed the answer to the pop quiz question.

6. Bryan washed his new sweater in hot water, and it shrinked.

7. Wind blowed down the old elm tree on the corner.

8. Mrs. Johnston teached me how to weave on a floor loom.

9. Taking his time, Sam drew a beautiful picture of a parrot.

10. The class plant growed nine inches during the summer.

11. My mother freezed the juice and maked popsicles.

12. Billy said, " I seed five deer in the park."

13. On the class trip, Lori buyed a souvenir agate.

Common and Proper Adjectives 1

An **adjective** is a word that describes a noun or a pronoun. Sometimes more than one adjective is used to describe one word. **Proper adjectives** are formed from proper nouns and are capitalized. **Common adjectives** are all other adjectives. They are not capitalized. (See *Write Source* page 590.)

Examples

The African crocodile can be dangerous. (*African* is a proper adjective.)

The green crocodile swam away. (*Green* is a common adjective.)

 **Directions** In the following sentences, some proper adjectives are not capitalized and some common adjectives are capitalized. Make the necessary changes. The first sentence has been done for you.

1. The ~~s~~outh ~~a~~merican anaconda is the world's ~~L~~argest snake.
   (S   A   l)

2. The african crocodile has a Pointed snout.

3. One of the most colorful reptiles is the Painted turtle.

4. The largest lizard in the world lives on komodo Island in the Pacific Ocean.

5. The only poisonous lizard in the united States lives in New Mexico.

6. Pythons are the Longest snakes in the world.

7. Can snakes move faster than a Running horse? The answer is no.

8. There are 27 different kinds of rattlesnakes on the north american continent.

Common and Proper Adjectives 2

Directions Read the sentences below, checking that proper adjectives are capitalized and that common adjectives are not. Make the necessary changes. The first sentence has been done for you. (See *Write Source* page 590.)

1. Of the $\overset{S}{\cancel{S}}$even continents, the $\overset{A}{\cancel{a}}$sian continent is the largest one.

2. The coldest continent is Antarctica.

3. The czech republic is located on the european continent.

4. African animal herds are larger than any other.

5. The european and the asian continents border each other in Russia.

6. Part of Antarctica, the ross Ice Shelf, is about the size of France.

7. Southern Asia has the world's Tallest peaks, in the himalayan Mountains.

8. The asian body of water called the Dead Sea is one of the saltiest places on earth.

9. The largest country in south America is Brazil.

10. Some of the most Dangerous waters in the world are found at the southern tip of the south american continent.

11. Australian animals such as the platypus and kangaroo are some of the most Unusual creatures in the world.

The Next Step Write a short paragraph about your state using both common and proper adjectives.

Demonstrative Adjectives

The **demonstrative adjectives**, *this, that, these,* and *those,* are used to point out specific nouns. *This* and *that* are used with singular nouns, while *these* and *those* are used with plural nouns. (See *Write Source* page 590.)

 Underline the demonstrative adjectives in the following sentences. If they are not used correctly, change them. The first one has been done for you.

this
1. The cold snap froze <u>these</u> bucket of water.

2. That plants lost their leaves because of the cold weather.

3. A gentle snowfall covered those steps overnight.

4. The cold air caused this bugs to hide under these woodpile.

5. These window has frost on it, but those window does not.

6. The temperature is 25 degrees according to this thermometer.

7. Is those thermometer Celsius or Fahrenheit?

8. These thermometer is Fahrenheit.

9. I didn't notice the frost on these spiderwebs yesterday.

10. That frost designs on the web are beautiful.

The Next Step Write four sentences about crayons using the demonstrative adjectives *this, that, these,* and *those.*

Forms of Adjectives

The **positive form** of an adjective describes a noun without comparing it to anyone or anything else. The **comparative form** of an adjective compares two people, places, things, or ideas. The **superlative form** compares three or more people, places, things, or ideas. (See *Write Source* page 592.)

Examples

Positive: Miguel is a fast runner.

Comparative: He is faster than anyone else on the team.

Superlative: He is the fastest runner in the league.

Positive: Sylvia is a skillful skateboarder.

Comparative: She is more skillful now than she was last year.

Superlative: She is now the most skillful skateboarder on her block.

(*More* and *most*, not *-er* and *-est,* are usually used with adjectives of two or more syllables.)

Directions   In the sentences below, write the correct form of the adjectives shown in parentheses.

1. I learned that diamond is the _____ mineral on earth. *(hard)*

2. Manuel's new shirt is made of _____ cotton. *(soft)*

3. Jill says that roses are _____ than daisies. *(beautiful)*

4. Frank is the _____ boy in his class and wants to play basketball. *(tall)*

5. Rubbing his hands together, Jon said, "It's getting _____." *(cold)*

6. Sue's twisted ankle was _____ today than yesterday. *(painful)*

7. The robins on the ground were the _____ sign of spring

    George had seen yet. *(hopeful)*

Adverbs

An **adverb** is a word that describes a verb, an adjective, or another adverb. Most adverbs answer when, where, or how questions. (See *Write Source* page 594.)

Example

Describing a Verb:
The kindergartners go **annually** to a farm.

   In the following sentences about field trips, circle the adverbs and underline the verbs they describe. The first sentence has been done for you. *Hint:* Sometimes more than one adverb in the same sentence can describe the same word.

1. The first-grade class (always) takes a trip to the zoo (early) in the fall.

2. Sometimes the second-grade class visits a local farm to pick apples.

3. The third grade usually travels down to the natural history museum

   and then writes a class report about endangered species.

4. Surprisingly, the fourth grade often votes for a field day to clean up the

   vacant lots in the neighborhood.

5. The fifth-grade class happily goes away to science camp for three days

   in the spring.

6. The sixth graders proudly march in the Earth Day parade.

7. In seventh grade, the students greatly enjoy the planetarium's special

   show about stars, comets, and the planets.

Types of Adverbs

Adverbs are used to modify verbs, adjectives, or other adverbs. Adverbs of time tell *when, how often,* or *how long* an action is done. Adverbs of place explain *where* something happens or *where* something is. Adverbs of manner say *how* something is done. Adverbs of degree show *how much* or *how little*. (See *Write Source* page 594.)

Examples

      Time: Jim crossed the street last. *(when)*

    Place: He crossed the street there. *(where)*

  Manner: He crossed the street quickly. *(how)*

  Degree: He crossed the street very quickly. *(how much)*

Directions   **Complete the sentences using the listed adverbs. The type of adverb to use for each sentence is given. The first one has been done for you.**

scarcely	inside	down	quickly
always	very	twice	cheerfully

1. On rainy days, Orin walks _____quickly_____ to school. *(manner)*

2. Even with an umbrella, he still gets _____ wet. *(degree)*

3. If the rainfall is heavy, he waits _____. *(place)*

4. Orin has been soaked _____ this month. *(time)*

5. He _____ keeps a dry change of clothes in his locker. *(time)*

6. Water from his wet clothes drips _____ on the floor. *(place)*

7. Orin is _____ bothered by the rain even if he gets wet. *(degree)*

8. He _____ says that we are 60 percent water anyway. *(manner)*

The Next Step On a piece of paper, make four columns. At the top of one put *time,* the next put *place,* the next write *manner,* and in the last write *degree.* Write as many adverbs as you can for each column. Compare papers with a classmate.

Forms of Adverbs

There are three forms of adverbs: the **positive** form, the **comparative** form, and the **superlative** form. (See page 596 in your *Write Source*. Make sure to note the special forms for *well* and *badly*.)

Examples

Positive:
I run swiftly and jump high.

Comparative:
He runs more swiftly and jumps higher.

Superlative:
She runs most swiftly and jumps highest.

Directions ▶ In each sentence, fill in the blanks with the correct forms of the adverb in *boldface*. The first sentence has been done for you.

1. Zoe did **well** on the test, but Jolene did _____*better*_____, and

   Bianca did the _____*best*_____ .

2. Jerry talks **fast,** but Yolanda talks _____, and

   Laurie talks the _____ .

3. We did **badly** in the race, but Mike's team did _____,

   and Georgia's team did the _____ .

4. Rolly swims **well,** but Lamarr swims _____, and

   Felix swims _____ of them all.

5. Angela climbed **carefully,** but Gary climbed _____,

   and Eric climbed _____ to the top of the climbing wall.

174

6. John studies **hard,** but Sharon studies _____ , and

   Tomas studies _____ of all.

7. Joanne speaks **clearly,** but Fumiko speaks _____ , and

   Sam speaks _____ during speeches.

8. Paloma sings **beautifully,** but Elena sings _____ , and

   Susan sings _____ .

Directions ▶ Fill in the comparative and superlative forms of the following adverbs. Then write sentences using all three forms of each adverb. (See *Write Source* page 596 for help.)

Positive Form	Comparative Form	Superlative Form
badly		
bravely		
late		
well		

1. (badly) _____

   _____

2. (bravely) _____

   _____

3. (late) _____

   _____

4. (well) _____

   _____

Prepositional Phrases 1

A **preposition** connects words to other words in a sentence. A preposition does not appear in a sentence by itself. A prepositional phrase gives more information. (See *Write Source* page 598.)

Example

Take a Walk in Their Shoes is a great book! (The word *in* is a preposition; the words *in Their Shoes* is a prepositional phrase.)

 Each book title below contains one preposition. Circle each preposition, and underline all the words in the prepositional phrase. The first one has been done for you.

1. (About) the B'Nai Bagels

2. Among the Volcanoes

3. A Blessing in Disguise

4. Boys at Work

5. Bridge to Terabithia

6. The Summer of the Swans

7. Journey into Terror

8. Little House on the Prairie

9. Sees Behind Trees

10. In the Language of Loons

11. Sybil Rides for Independence

12. Diary of a Drummer Boy

13. A Letter to Amy

14. When I Was Young in the Mountains

15. Song of the Trees

16. Arthur for the Very First Time

17. On the Riverbank

18. Sweet Rhymes Around the World

19. Sideways Stories from Wayside School

20. If You Grew Up with George Washington

Prepositional Phrases 2

Directions In the paragraph below, underline all the prepositions and double underline the rest of the prepositional phrase. The first one has been done for you.

1   Jake noticed that new tires eventually wear thin. His

2   father told him that the tires get worn away <u>by</u> <u><u>the road</u></u>. Jake

3   knew that there are millions of cars wearing their tires out

4   all the time. He wondered why he didn't see huge piles of tire

5   tread along the highways. Where did all of that rubber go? So

6   Jake went to the library, and he read articles on the Internet.

7   He discovered that carmakers and others had asked this same

8   question. They were worried that airborne tire tread might be

9   harmful to people's health. Jake learned that the tread breaks

10   into tiny pieces. Wind, rain, and sun help break down those little

11   pieces even more. Very little of the tire tread stays in the air.

12   Even the rubber dust in the air doesn't stay there long. The tiny

13   pieces of tire tread blow away or become part of the ground. Jake

14   told his father about his special studies. His father was impressed.

The Next Step Look around your classroom. Select an object. Describe its location with as many prepositional phrases as you can. See if a partner can figure out the object you selected.

Coordinating Conjunctions

A **coordinating conjunction** connects equal parts of a sentence: two or more words, two or more phrases, or two or more clauses. The coordinating conjunctions are *and, but, or, nor, for, so,* and *yet.* (See *Write Source* page 600.)

Examples

Connecting Words: Mugs **and** Barney barked.

Connecting Phrases: Kat ran out the door **and** into the yard.

Connecting Clauses: Kat kept running, **and** Mugs followed.

Directions ▶ Circle all the coordinating conjunctions in the following paragraph.

1   When I was little, I was scared of the dark. I thought

2   monsters or ghosts would come out and yell, "Boo!" I imagined

3   closets hiding goblins or wild animals. Finally, I got a night-light,

4   and it worked like a charm. It was shaped like a seashell, and

5   I could see its friendly glow in the dark. It lit up my room a

6   little, so I could sleep better. Through the years, I enjoyed having

7   my night-light right next to my bed. Now I am older, and I don't

8   need it anymore.

 On the center of the lines below, copy some of the coordinating conjunctions you circled. On either side, write the words, phrases, or clauses that each conjunction connects. Two have been done for you.

1. _____

2. _____

3. ____ I got a night-light,   and   it worked like a charm. ____

4. It lit up my room a little,   so   I could sleep better. ____

5. _____

The Next Step Choose another student sample from your text or something from your own writing folder. Find five phrases or clauses that contain coordinating conjunctions and write them here.

1. _____

_____

2. _____

_____

3. _____

_____

4. _____

_____

5. _____

_____

© Great Source. All rights reserved. (4)

Subordinating Conjunctions

A **subordinating conjunction** connects two clauses to make a complex sentence. The subordinating conjunction may come at the beginning or in the middle of the sentence. (See *Write Source* page 600.)

Examples

After we went to the game, we stopped for ice cream.

We stopped for ice cream after we went to the game.

 **Circle the subordinating conjunction in each sentence below. The first one has been done for you.**

1. (Because) I missed the bus, I was late for school.

2. We play soccer in this park after school lets out.

3. We'll have to go inside if we see lightning.

4. We can't go swimming until the rain stops.

5. I won't finish my homework unless I start soon.

6. While I clean our room, Polly will walk the dog.

7. When I finish my homework, I'll call Sam.

8. Juanita couldn't come to school because she is sick.

9. Since it is dark, I don't want to walk home alone.

10. I like my aunt because she is funny.

11. Before we moved, I went to a different school.

Directions  From the previous exercise, choose three sentences that have subordinating conjunctions at the beginning. Rewrite each sentence so the subordinating conjunction is in the middle.

Examples

Because I missed the bus, I was late for school.

I was late for school because I missed the bus.

1. _____

_____

2. _____

_____

3. _____

_____

Directions  Now choose three sentences that have subordinating conjunctions in the middle. Rewrite each sentence so the subordinating conjunction is at the beginning.

1. _____

_____

2. _____

_____

3. _____

_____

Conjunctions Review

This activity is a review of coordinating and subordinating conjunctions.

 **Directions** ▶ **Each sentence below has one coordinating conjunction and one subordinating conjunction. Underline both, and write "C" above each coordinating conjunction and "S" above each subordinating conjunction. The first sentence has been done for you.**

1. My sister <u>and</u> I washed our dog <u>after</u> he rolled in the mud.
   (C above "and", S above "after")

2. We could play basketball or go roller-skating unless it's too cold.

3. Jerry has to change clothes and clean his room before he can play.

4. We went to the mall, yet we couldn't find the store where we had seen the video game.

5. Though it was almost time for dinner, we ate grapes and cheese.

6. We're not hungry, but we'll eat if you're having pizza!

7. Stephanie and I walked to the museum after we rode the bus downtown.

8. Jim or Amir can feed the fish while Sandy waters the plants.

9. I want to watch TV, but I can't unless I finish my homework.

10. Because it's raining, my mom or dad will pick me up.

11. Although Heather had a cat, she still wanted a parakeet and a lovebird.

12. After my birthday party, I wanted to write and send all my thank-you notes by e-mail.

Directions ▸ Add the needed conjunctions to the sentences below.

1. _____ it's 9:00, Lilly _____ James are still sleeping.

2. It's Tuesday, _____ practice is canceled_____ it's raining.

3. My dad honked the horn, _____ the cow stayed in the road

   _____ another car came along.

4. _____ the boots seemed big enough, John could not get them on

   his feet.

5. Sue laughed out loud _____ rolling in the snow.

6. Mom _____ Dad will make some hot chocolate _____ the

   sledding party.

7. Luann didn't feel well, _____ she drank some tea _____

   took a nap.

Interjections

An **interjection** is a word or phrase used to express strong emotion or surprise. A comma or an exclamation point sets off an interjection from the rest of the sentence. (See *Write Source* page 602.)

Examples

Yikes! The cat's in the top tree branches!

Did you hear that motorcycle? Wow!

Watch where you're going, hey!

Man, that's dangerous!

Fill in the blanks in the paragraph below with interjections from the list. The first one has been done for you.

Boy	Well	Good point	Wait	Oh no
Help	Wrong	My goodness	Wow	Yikes

1 Do you know that the world's fastest plane can fly 2,000

2 miles per hour? _____*Wow*_____! I could fly across the country in

3 an hour and a half. If I didn't want to fly, how fast could I go?

4 _____, the world's fastest train in Japan can reach 190 miles

5 per hour. _____! Everything outside the windows

6 would look blurry. I bet cars can't go that fast. _____! A

7 company in Germany can change a regular sports car so it can

8 reach 210 miles per hour. _____, no one can legally drive

9 that speed in this country. _____, I am glad that's true. How

10 could you ever cross the street? _____!

Parts of Speech Review 1

This activity is a review of all the parts of speech you have studied. Do the activity with a partner if your teacher allows it.

 **Each list below contains words that are examples of one part of speech. Label each list with the name of the correct part of speech.**

1. _____

    dog
    book
    California
    idea
    mechanic

4. _____

    run
    said
    throw
    write
    were

7. _____

    I
    you
    their
    his
    anyone

2. _____

    quickly
    loudly
    well
    carefully
    down

5. _____

    big
    tall
    tallest
    smart
    an

8. _____

    of
    at
    to
    over
    on top of

3. _____

    and
    or
    but
    because
    although

6. _____

    Hey!
    Oh!
    Wow!
    Yikes!
    Yes!

Parts of Speech Review 2

This activity is a review of all the parts of speech you have studied.

 **Directions** — Read the following fable. Above each underlined word, write the correct part of speech. The first two have been done for you.

The Ant and the Dove

1   One <u>day</u>, an ant <u>crawled</u> to a little pond to have a drink.

2   When <u>he</u> was almost to the pond's edge, he <u>fell</u> down the <u>slippery</u>

3   bank into the <u>water</u>. The ant was about to drown when a <u>dove</u>

4   <u>saw</u> him. The dove <u>quickly</u> picked up a <u>leaf</u> and dropped it into

5   the pond. The ant climbed onto the leaf and drifted <u>safely</u> back

6   to land. As he <u>stepped</u> off the leaf, the ant looked up <u>and</u> saw a

7   hunter who was taking aim <u>at</u> the dove with his gun. The <u>tiny</u>

8   ant scurried up the hunter's boot and bit the hunter hard on the

9   leg. The hunter yelled, "<u>Ouch!</u>" When the dove heard <u>him</u>, it flew

10   away. The <u>moral</u> of the story is "One good turn deserves another."

Parts of Speech Review 3

This activity reviews all the parts of speech you have studied.

Directions

Read the following paragraph. Write the underlined words in the correct columns below.

I recently <u>saw</u> an old picture of a <u>suburb</u> of <u>Milwaukee</u>, <u>Wisconsin</u>. <u>Because</u> the photo <u>was</u> 100 years old, <u>it</u> was black and white. <u>Where</u> tall pine <u>trees</u> once <u>proudly</u> stood, huge <u>electrical</u> towers <u>now</u> <u>stretch</u> <u>their</u> metal branches <u>to</u> the sky. Once a simple dirt path lead <u>through</u> the trees, <u>but</u> it has expanded <u>into</u> four-lane roads <u>and</u> broad <u>concrete</u> sidewalks. <u>Wow!</u> A quiet rural area <u>turned</u> into a <u>very</u> <u>busy</u> city.

Nouns **Verbs** **Pronouns**

_____ _____ _____

_____ _____ _____

_____ _____ _____

_____ _____ _____

Adverbs **Adjectives** **Prepositions**

_____ _____ _____

_____ _____ _____

Interjections **Conjunctions**

_____ _____ _____

_____ _____